'The Coming Global Fascist State"

by
Friends and lovers of Freedom

Robert M.Wettergreen

Copyright © 2012 Rob M. Wettergreen

The rights of the author of the Work have been asserted by him.

All rights reserved. No part of this publication may be reproduced, stored in a retrieval system, or transmitted, in any form or by any means, without the prior written permission of the publisher or the author, nor be otherwise circulated in any form of binding or cover other than that in which it is published and without a similar condition being imposed on the subsequent purchaser.

ISBN: 978-1-920315-76-4

Just Done Productions
Publishing
Durban
2012

publish@justdone.co.za
http://www.justdone.co.za
International: http://www.Lulu.com/JustDone

PROLOGUE

Using the analogue of sleep and deception it is only when you wake up that you know that you have been asleep! So it is with deception! You need to know what is going on in order not to be deceived.

Unbeknown to most there is a war going on, involving a deception so great, so utterly shameless, so totally ruthless that undoubtedly it is the "World's Greatest Scam."

What is going on is going to affect every living soul and it is vital that people wake up and take note before it is too late! This cannot be ignored.

People are going to be deceived, vast multitudes of them will be deceived into receiving the Mark of the Beast………give them a copy of this!

'LEST YE KNOW'….A GRAVE THREAT THAT PEOPLE NEED TO KNOW ABOUT

How many are aware that the supposedly well intentioned Treaty on 'Climate Change' proposed at the 2009 United Nations Climate Change Conference in Copenhagen actually stated in it's 200 page wording that a 'World Government' would be created. The word government actually appeared as the first of three purposes for the new entity. The second purpose was the transfer of wealth from the West to third world countries in satisfaction of what was 'coyly' put as a 'climate debt' for creating and causing the CO_2 problem. The third purpose was enforcement. If the treaty had been signed, legally it would even have taken precedence over the Constitution of the United States.

If the U.S. President had signed the treaty it would

have ended America's freedom, democracy and prosperity forever - <u>that is how close it came</u> and provides a very clear indication of the impatience of its sponsors to put a World Government in place and also how ready they are! Unknown to ordinary people the ones behind the scene trying to impose the World Order Government are some of the most powerful individuals and groups in the world.

<u>This was Part of A Warning To America by Lord Monckton, a former adviser to Lady Margaret Thatcher</u> who spoke at Bethel University in St. Paul, MN (10/4/09) on the UN Climate Change Treaty that was scheduled to be signed in December 2009. Lord Monckton was hosted by the Minnesota Free Market Institute.[1][2]

The Climate Change Conference (COPE 17) held in Durban, South Africa from 28th November to December 9th. stated aims were to secure agreement on the future of the Kyoto Protocol and to finalize the exact provisions of the US$100 billion long-term Green Climate Fund that the previous Convention in Cancun, Mexico agreed would come into effect in 2010. Governments would also need to agree on a broader framework to reduce greenhouse gases under the Climate Change Convention.

After exhaustive negotiations that continued well into the early hours of the morning at the end of the Durban Convention, COP17 President, Maite Nkoana-Mashabane, South Africa's Minister of International relations announced that the sought after agreements had been reached and <u>declared the C</u>onvention a success. Also, that details of the

1 Text thanks to Gary Jacobucci
2 Lord Monckton's *Warning To America* www.rense.com

final agreements would be announced at a later date once legal processes had been finalized. The next Climate Change Conference is scheduled to be held in Qatar late 2012.

Is what we are seeing the 'stepping stone approach' that was used in the establishment of the European Union where opposition and public outcry was overcome by taking such incremental steps? To get foot in the door "free-trade areas" were initially offered and expanded upon until the European Union was born.

What Cope 17 however, did secure was the unanimous agreement of the majority of the over 190 nations delegates attending the conference that the U.N.'s initiative and the lead it had taken in the fight against Global Warming had to be followed byall nations. Likely this 'group power' approach will be employed in overriding the objections of individual (nations).

The question now is whether it will succeed in bringing about the long sought after 'World Order' Government, when all such attempts up until now have failed? This we shall soon find out, for at this late hour, likely little can be done to change matters – so prepared we should be! On June 23, 2011 Independent Online[3] carried a report that the UN had given South Africa R200 million towards hosting the event indicating the importance of the event to the UN .

Certainly the Bible tells in Revelation Chapter 13 that there will be a World Government under the United Nations – this is indelibly written in Scripture. Likely it will be imposed upon those developed nations not in favor by sheer weight of numbers. In other words by a 'majority decision' of

---

3   www.iol.co.za

lesser nations put across as a non-negotiable international obligation for the common good!

Might it also be said that we are now living in 'borrowed time' and that the World Order Government that was intended to be put in place soon after the millennium that fortuitously was delayed by the War in Iraq lasting six years instead of the six months the was originally planned and further delayed by the collapse of the financial markets and the recession that followed, will soon become a reality? There are compelling reasons by its sponsors for the world government to be implemented without delay and yes even before the end of 2012. So it is imperative that the world's hopelessly deceived people wake up!

'Carbon isotope C_{12} C_{13} concentration ratios in the atmosphere, measured accurately with an isotope ratio mass spectrometer; show that only 4% of atmospheric CO_2 originate from fossil fuel burning. The Earth has had warming and cooling periods throughout its history and CO_2 increases have followed temperature increases for thousands of years.[4]

So, was COPE 17 and the entire 'climate change' debate really no more than a futile nitpicking about the responsibility for the 4% fossil fuel carbon emissions and their effect on global temperature rise? Or is there another side to the story that is being missed?

Could it be that 'Global Warming' is in fact more about the Biblical Maledictions referred to in Deuteronomy 28? Where in verse 23....there is a warning by God that.....'*your skies will become as copper and the ground as iron.*

24. Your God will give powder and dust as rain........the

[4] J David Raal, Emeritus Professor UKZN *The Mercury*, November 11, 2011

warnings continue on until verse 68 and are pretty graphic. Why would theologians be silent about this, surely such dire warnings cannot be ignored and demand some attention?

So is 'climate change,' just a guise? Is it not about control, the ultimate form of control, a global fascist church state as alluded to by Lord Monckton? Notice something about the U.N. that is not commonly known;

'The Constitution of the U.S.S.R. is almost identical to the Constitution of the United Nations....' All nations will be brought under it's, the U.N.'s 'iron-fisted' fascist control. [5]

No one will enter the New World Order unless he or she will make a <u>pledge to worship Lucifer</u>. No one will enter the New Age unless he will take a Luciferian initiation. The light reveals to us the presence of the Christ comes from Lucifer. He is the light-giver, he is aptly named the 'Morning Star' because it is his light that heralds for man the dawn of a great consciousness. [6]

How could this characterize the UN which supposedly was setup to end to wars and bring peace and prosperity to all nations?

People need to know that the United Nations was actually brought into existence by the Illuminati. They had tried and failed with the League of Nations after World War I and so they engineered the Second World War to batter nations into agreeing to replace it with the United Nations. They wrote the charter that would make the UN a stalking horse for a fully-fledged world government.

---

5   *Fourth Reich of the Rich*. Emissary Publishers, South Pasadena, Ca 1978 p.140 . (notice on page 15 the current situation regarding the Greman Second Reich)

6   David Spangler, Director of Planetary Initiation, UN

Also, noteworthy is that the Illuminati's control of money translates into them controlling the world. The problems of poverty, debt, war are made to happen because it makes humanity easier to control.

Might this be a wake-up call for folk to start seeing and to take seriously what is really going on in the world and also to properly **understand and expose the churches involvement which is key to the entire matter?**

SATAN HAS USED RELIGION, THE CHURCH AS A FRONT AND DISGUISE AND COVER BEHIND WHICH TO OPERATE AND IT WASN'T LONG AFTER THE LAST OF THE APOSTLES FELL ASLEEP IN DEATH THAT HIS INFILTRATION OF THE CHURCH BEGAN. THIS WAS ACHIEVED THROUGH A COMBINING OF CHURCH AND STATE AND THE BEGINNING OF THE 'HOLY ROMAN EMPIRE.'

The legally recognized supremacy of the Pope began in 538 A.D. when there went into effect a decree of Emperor Justinian, making the Bishop of Rome head over all the churches, the definer of doctrine and the corrector of heretics.

Vigilicus ascended the papacy in 538 A.D. under the military protection of Baliserius.[7]

THE BIBLE WARNED THAT THIS WOULD HAPPEN. NOTICE THIS IN 2 THESSALONIANS 2.2,...... 'THE DAY OF THE LORD IS HERE.

3. LET NO ONE SEDUCE YOU...IT (THAT DAY) WILL NOT COME UNLESS THE APOSTASY COMES FIRST AND THE MAN OF LAWLESSNESS GETS REVEALED, THE SON OF DESTRUCTION.

---

7 *History of the Christian Church* vol. 3 p. 327

4. HE IS IN OPPOSITION AND LIFTS HIMSELF UP OVER EVERYONE WHO IS CALLED "GOD" AN OBJECT OF REVERENCE, SO THAT HE SITS DOWN IN THE TEMPLE OF GOD PUBLICLY SHOWING HIMSELF TO BE A GOD.

The Pope is not only the representative of Jesus Christ, but he is Jesus Christ himself, hidden under the veil of flesh.[8]

And God himself is obliged to abide by the Judgments of His priests, and whether or not to pardon.

'Receive the Tiara, be ordained with the triple crown and know thou art the Father of princes and kings, victor of the whole world, <u>replacement of Jesus Christ</u> and receive the glory and honour that has no end and belongs to you.[9]

However, Satan knows that his time as 'ruler of the world' is up, but is still as determined as ever to win by having the entire world made to bow down to him. <u>His mindset is that because he is destined to go into destruction, that he will take all humanity down with him at Armageddon, to leave God with an empty victory.</u> In other words if he cannot have the world and all its glory, neither will God! In effect humanity is being held as a ransom!

Why would such critically important information not be forthcoming from the church? Obviously, it would blow apart and undo the guise and cover that Satan has used to mislead and deceive the world. The church is run in such a way that the laity are not permitted to know anything about what is going on deep inside the church nor are they permitted to read the Bible?

On the face of it the Church is a hugely prestigious <u>organization,</u> immaculate in every respect, spread out

8   *Catholic National*, July, 1895
9   Morgan Thomas, *Pontiff*, p. 332

across the world with many fine cathedral's and buildings, wonderfully well run and efficient hospitals, schools, universities managed and run by an army of upright, loyal people dedicated to caring for the flock, the 'faithful' and it would be absolutely preposterous to suggest that this is all part of a cover behind which Satan 'operates,' were it not true.

The last place anyone would suspect to find Satan is in the church and yet there he is with all religion now under his control. If the Bible tells this to be so and if <u>the Late Pope John Paul II would actually confirm this</u>, as do the other clergy that are mentioned, we had better believe it.

So take a closer look at how the Bible explains how this great deception is being carried out.

Notice the following scriptures and the various Biblical characters that are involved; Revelation 13: 3, 4.....***all the world*** *wondered after the beast and they worshipped the dragon (Satan) which gave the power and authority unto the beast. (the Papacy)* Here Satan the Great Dragon - is shown in his role as world ruler, empowering the Papacy, the church – but we need to take an even closer look to see how it all works;

Satan has a network and God has one;

<u>God's Network;</u> Service to God and Studying his Word, Service to man and Evangelizing His Word

<u>Satan's Network;</u> Sport, Magazines, Sex, Porn, Music, Parties, drugs, alcohol, tobacco, homosexuality, Spiritualism, Secret Societies, Work, Wealth.

This is the system that we are living in today, setup to preoccupy us so that we will fail to recognize the signs of

the times and thus succumb to Satanic Deception that will end up destroying us!

To throw a little more light on what we are up against notice the following extracts of the inscriptions on the 'Emerald tablets of Toth' claimed to date back 36,000 years and alleged to have been found beneath a Mayan temple in Mexico in 1925 and translated by Maurice Doreal;

'Forth came they into this cycle, formless were they, of another vibration, existing unseen to the children of earth-men.'

- *'Yet beware, the serpent Unseen they walk among thee in places where the rites have been said; <u>again as time passes, shall they take the semblance of men.</u>'*

'Sought they from the kingdom of the shadows , to destroy man and rule in his place –

Also, notice what follows; *"Seek not the kingdom of shadows, for evil will surely appear,* **for only the <u>master of brightness</u> shall conquer the shadow of fear."**

"Know ye, O brother, that fear is an obstacle great; be master of all in brightness, the shadow will disappear...heed my wisdom, the voice of LIGHT is clear."[10]

Don Juan, the Mexican Indian shaman, tells Carlos Castaneda the following:

"We have a predator that came from the depths of the cosmos and took over the rule of our lives. Human beings are its prisoners. If we protest, it suppresses our protest. If we act independently, it demands we do not....

"No, no, no, no," [Carlos replies] "this is absurd Don Juan.

---

10   The entire content of the tablets is available on the website: http://crystalinks.com/emerald.html. or in the book *The Emerald Tablets of Toth* – Atlantean Source Books, Nashville, Tennessee.

What you are saying is monstrous. It simply cannot be true."

"Why not?" don Jaun asks calmly. "Why not? Because it infuriates you?

"There are no more dreams for man but the dreams of an animal who is being raised to become a piece of meat: trite, conventional, imbecilic."[11]

Being relatively few in number the Anunnaki - An, Lucifer or Satan and his demons, the extraterrestrials invaders of the planet need the Illuminati as a front for them to carry out their agenda for the creation of a planetary dictatorship with us humans as a type of micro-chipped robotic mind controlled slave population.

These reptilians have been working to regain control of the planet they believe is theirs. Sumerian tablets dating back to around 3500BC tell of the arrival of the Annunnaki who interbred with Earth races to create bloodlines through which to manipulate the world while appearing to be human.

The book of Dzyan tells of a reptilian race it calls the Sarpa or Dragons who came from skies to bring civilization to the earth. It's leader was called the Great Dragon. The same was true in China of the Lung Wang or 'Dragon Kings' who were described as part human, part serpent.

Nagas were described as a very advanced race or species and the offspring from the interbreeding of humans with serpent gods. The Nagas intermingled with the 'white people' to produce a reptilian-mammal hybrid that became...*the Aryan kings*! These are the same bloodlines that ruled the Sumerian Empire, Egypt, Babylon, Greece, Rome and today's

---

11   Castaneda, 1988

Anglo-American duel world power!

Indian legend says that the Nagas could take human or reptilian form at will. This is referred to by UFO ET fraternity as 'shape-shifting.' Buddha is claimed to have been of the royal line of the Nagas as were the Chinese emperors.

Satan the Adversary is described in The Hebrew Torah as the 'Old Serpent' or Dragon' and the ruler of the Nefilim who fled within the earth after losing a cosmic battle for supremacy.

Notice how this is confirmed in the New Testament in the Book of Revelations 12.7....*And war broke out in Heaven: Michael and his angels battled with the dragon, and the dragon and its angels battled.*

8. It did not prevail.....

9.so down the great dragon was hurled, the original serpent, called Devil and Satan who is misleading the entire earth and his angels were hurled down with him.

12. ...be glad you heavens. Woe for the earth...because the Devil has come down to you, having great anger, knowing he has a short period of time.

We are almost there, either we bring this hidden dictatorship to an end and enter God's Millennium of Peace or God forbid we face a future in a global fascist state.

CONTENTS

Prologue	Iii
1. Our Unseen Enemy	1
2. The Mayflower	3
4. Rome And The Real Power Behind The Pope (Die Romse Gevaar)	7
5. Ecumenism	9
6. Looking Inside Religion	14
7. Masonry	27
8. A Warning By The Late Pope John Paul Ii	30
9. Satan's Rigged System – The Secular World That Is Ruining The Earth	33
10. A War About Worship	37
11. God's People Israel	40
12. Israel And The Nations	45
14. The World's Greatest Scam	50
15. Two Vitally Important Scriptures	55
16. A World Order Government	57
17. Climate Change Hijacked?	61
18. The Un - A Provisional Entity!	63
19. 'Commanders Of Israel'	65
20. 'You Peter' ….. A Satanic Deception	67

21. 'A Happy Ending?' Only You Can Make That Happen!   70

22. Other Views   73

1. OUR UNSEEN ENEMY

The Bible tells the end of a matter to help strengthen our faith. So, who is this 'unseen enemy of mankind? Notice please, the end of this enemy of God and of all mankind found in Isaiah Chapter 14; 12 -17.

"To the Heavens I shall go up. Above the Stars of God I shall lift up my throne...

14. I shall make myself resemble the Most High."

15. "However, down to Sheol you will be brought, to the remotest parts of the pit.

16 Those seeing you will gaze even at you; ......saying 'Is this the man that was agitating the earth, that was making kingdoms rock,

17. that made the productive land like a wilderness and overthrew its very cities...

This is no fictional cartoon character as he is often depicted, the cute two horned character dressed in red with pitch fork in hand, no this is the one who was hurled to the earth with a third of the angels of heaven who are now demon's and he is very active in his role as 'Ruler of the World' as confirmed by Jesus in John 14.30.

SATAN CANNOT OPENLY GET THE WORLD TO BOW DOWN TO HIM, SO HE USES RELIGION, THE CHURCH AS A FRONT, AS A DISGUISE OR COVER FROM BEHIND WHICH TO OPERATE AND IT WASN'T LONG AFTER THE LAST OF THE APOSTLES FELL ASLEEP IN DEATH THAT HIS INFILTRATION OF THE CHURCH BEGAN. JESUS WARNED THAT THIS WOULD HAPPEN!

Satan knows that his time as 'ruler of the world' is up, but is still as determined as ever to win by having the entire world made to bow down to him. His mindset is that if he is destined to go into destruction, then he will take all humanity down with him at Armageddon, to leave God with an empty victory. In other words if he cannot have the world and all it's glory, neither will God!

Revelation 13: 7 tells that...... *the beast (Antichrist) was granted to make war with the saints and overcame them....* the Inquisition.

THE INQUISITION

The Catholic Church is a respecter of conscience and of liberty....Nevertheless when confronted with heresy she has recourse to force, to corporeal punishment, to torture...she lit in Italy the funeral piles of the Inquisition. [1]

<u>Experience tells us that there is no other remedy for evil, but to put heretics (Protestants) to death</u>; for the (Romesh) church proceeded gradually and then tried every remedy. At first she merely excommunicated them; afterwards she added a fine; then she banished them; and finally she was constrained to put them to death.[2]

So according to the Church taking a stand for the Bible is evil and warrants Death. How ironic if it were not for the truth about what's going on deep inside the church! Surely this should not be allowed to continue?

---

1   Alfred Baudrillart 'T*he Catholic Church Renaissance and Protestantism*' p. 182 – 183
2   Cardinal Bellarmine – an estimated 100 million Christians were killed during the middle ages. Some put the figure higher at 170 million!

2. THE MAYFLOWER

For 1260 years in fulfilment of prophecy the Church of Rome has tried to destroy Christianity by removing the Bible, by destroying it's people, causing many to flee as was the case of those who boarded the 'Mayflower.' and who helped make the United States the 'land of the free.' [3]

Hunted, persecuted and imprisoned they could discern no future of better days and many yielded to the conviction that for such as would serve God according to the dictates of their conscience, England was ceasing to be a habitable place.

<u>In Europe the Papacy had taken control and through it the Jesuit Order, and in a most diabolical way was persecuting anybody who stood for the Bible.</u>

It is also written that ...... when God's hand seemed pointing them across the sea to a land where they might found for themselves a state and to leave for their children the precious heritage of religious liberty they went forward without shrinking in the path of Providence. [4]

The Mayflower in 1620 – The Pilgrims reached the coast of what is now Massachusetts on Dec 21, 1620. They named their little settlement 'Plymouth' after the city that they had sailed from in England. [5]

This was a happy little place for them – now they were free. They could build a country based on two core principles, the one – Religious Freedom and freedom from <u>the Monarchy </u>and Separation of Church and State.

3   *History of New England* Chapter 3 paragraph 43
4   *The Great Controversy.* Ellen White p. 291
5   Wikipedia

'We hold these truths to be self evident that all men are created equal, that they are endowed by the Creator with certain inalienable rights, that among these are Life, Liberty and the Pursuit of Happiness.' [6]

'Congress shall make no law respecting the establishment of religion or prohibiting the free exercise thereof.'[7]

These two statements are the very Foundation's upon which the United States of America was built; 'Freedom from the Inquisition and the oppression of the Papacy'

At the moment America is a democracy - the government is however, leaning more and more to becoming fascist.

One of the many indications of this would be that there would have to be a majority in the U.S. Government that will lean out and drive America to accept the laws of Rome.

An extremely important example of this can be seen in the present membership of the U.S. Supreme Court ....Justices - Roberts, Kennedy, Scalia, Thomas & Alito.... 5 in number or (56%) – are Catholics **and for the first time in U.S. history, Catholics are the majority in the U.S. Justice system.** How can this not influence judicial decisions across America and in fact corrupt and destroy the fidelity, integrity and the very fabric of the entire Justice System of the United States? Again, this is just one very small example of what is going on. For all intents and purposes it could be said that America is now very much a Catholic country.

Are the Federal immigration judges not responsible for this, responsible for turning the land of the free into a province of Rome, otherwise who else?

---

6   *American Declaration of Independence*, 1776.
7   *Constitution of the United States of America*, 1789.

3. AMERICA IN A NEW ROLE

So, while the United States was set up like a godly institution, Satan would find a way to infiltrate it and twist it so that America would become Rome's law enforcer.

Notice America, in her role as the Biblical false prophet in Revelation 13.11 .....*I beheld another beast and he had two horns like a lamb and he spake as a dragon.....*

So we have the first beast, the Antichrist (Papacy) that came out of the sea (the people) and now a second beast rises out of the earth – (an unpopulated area.) The Bible gives the identity of the Second Beast!

The Bible says a second beast would arise from the earth that would enforce laws of the first beast – according to the Bible if you do not bow down, you will be killed – we are coming to a time of great tribulation – you may not recognize it now.

But Revelation 13:11 sounds a warning ....*this beast (the Biblical 'False Prophet' America) spoke like a dragon (Satan)* Somehow this nation will start talking like Satan. <u>This American power that was founded by Protestants running away from Rome – is going to speak like a dragon and take the world back to Rome</u>.

Revelation 13:12....*he exercises all the power of the first beast before him and causeth the earth and they which dwell thereon to worship the beast whose deadly wound was healed.* <u>It will drive the entire world to bow down to the first beast (the papacy.)</u> It is through the church that worship is directed to Satan. How this will happen will be explained as we continue.

In Revelation 13: 3, 4 we see that.....*all the world wondered after the beast, And they worshipped the dragon (Satan) which gave the power and authority unto the beast. (the Papacy)*

By following Antichrist (the Papacy) we are automatically channeling worship to the Dragon (Satan). This has gradually been gaining momentum and unknown to most it is being done through Ecumenism, the whole world is now being made to bow to Rome in order that worship may be channeled to the dragon. Satan needs the entire world to bow down to Him to prove the challenge he made against God's Sovereignty and right to rule in Eden. But this will be to no avail as according to the Bible in Revelation 12.11 the battle has already been won by those unsung hero's who did not 'love their souls' even in the face of death, but he will nevertheless persist with his agenda until he is stopped.

So certainly, we can expect the return of God's triumphant Son and our King Jesus in Great Power and Glory at anytime. Also, know that God will not allow Satan's wicked system to continue a day longer than justice deserves. As such we can only speculate that this would be the reason that God will allow Satan to put his world government in place! In fact the Bible clearly tells that there will be a world government. What will this government be like?

'The Constitution of the U.S.S.R is almost identical to the Constitution of the United Nations....' All nations will be brought under it's, the U.N.'s 'iron-fisted' fascist control. [8]

---

8   *Fourth Reich of the Rich*. Emissary Publishers, South Pasadena, Ca 1978 p.140. (notice on page 15 the current situation regarding the Second Reich)

4. ROME AND THE REAL POWER BEHIND THE POPE (DIE ROMSE GEVAAR)

Revelation 13.14.....it misleads those who dwell on the earth....

15...and there was granted to it to give breath to the image of the wild beast (U.N.) so that the image of the wild beast (the UN) should both speak and cause to be killed all who will not worship the image of the wild beast.

16 And it puts under compulsion all persons ....that they should have a mark on the right hand and forehead.

17 that nobody might buy or sell except a person having the mark of the wild beast or the number of its name.

18.....it is a man's number; and its number is six hundred and sixty six.

The letters inscribed on the Pope's miter are these 'Vicarius Fili Dei' which translated from Latin is VICAR OF THE SON OF GOD. By adding up the letters of this name using Roman numerals, the number of the name will be 666.[9]

Vicarius - 'Substituting for or in the place of...'

V I C A R I U S
$5 + 1 + 100 + 0 + 0 + 1 + 5 + 0 =$ 112

F I L I I
$0 + 1 + 50 + 1 + 1 =$ 53

D E I
$500 + 0 + 1 =$ $\underline{501}$
          666

---

9   *Our Sunday Visitor*, April 18, 1915

It's [the Jesuit's Order's] objective was, and is still to destroy the effects of the Reformation and to re-establish the Holy Roman Empire.¹⁰

It's aim is to take the Inquisition to a new level – the head of the Inquisition while Paul II was in power – was Cardinal Ratzinger who is now Pope Benedict XVI.

A leopard does not change it's spots – there's going to be a repeat of the Inquisition...soon! The persecution that is coming will be horrific beyond belief and understanding where millions, if not billions are going to be killed. It's victims will be Protestant Christians, in fact all who refuse to accept the 'Mark of the Beast.'

The New World Order government was due for implementation soon after the turn of the century, but was likely delayed by the War in Iraq becoming protracted and lasting six years instead of the six months that was planned. The crash of the financial markets further delayed matters. But with that all behind it could be upon us at any time, it is long overdue and it certainly will not be going away, according to the Scriptures there will be a World Order Government! As such it would indeed appear that we are now into 'borrowed' time!

A former New-ager Randall Bair, states those who refuse the mark of the beast will be targeted for extermination in what would euphemistically be called re-education centres of love and relocation, that is death camps in disguise.¹¹

---

10   Leo H Lehmann, 1942 *American Historian Behind the Dictators*, New York, Agora Publishing Co., p. 26
11   '*Exposing the New Age*' by Randall Bair, 1989

5. ECUMENISM

Ecumenism is the greatest threat to Christianity, it puts Christ on the same level as false Gods.

In 2005 the Anti Christ was calling for Ecumenism, a coming together of the world's religion's (including the mainline churches – this has already happened), to be made a priority – like ancient Babylon, all the world to be made One – but that was Unity in Error - Christ also wanted unity, but unity in truth and love.

In an ecumenical world (the Son of Man had to be removed) so that you can go refer to Krishna, to anyone to save the world. We are after-all, waiting for our Cosmic Christ, are we not? Definitely not Jesus.

The UN is leading us to a One World Religion – In the name of World Religion the UN appears to have embraced a sort of religious universalism that views all religions as equals and is seeking to ban proselytizing.

No Christian Bibles are welcome at the UN because you can't be saved by the blood of Jesus. Jesus has to be taken off His throne and put down.

This is not intended to vilify ones church, or religion, but simply to state facts that should not be allowed to be ignored and quietly swept under the rug. Clearly, this is something that the American people need to know, if the freedoms and liberties for which America stands are to be preserved!

When the United States rules the World, the Catholic Church will rule the world. [12]

---

12 Archbishop Quigley 1903, *The Chicago Tribune*.

This war is about worship and who it is that must be worshipped. It is a continuation of the war that happened in heaven and is continuing here on earth.

Here the agenda comes to fore – again it's Unity in Error – Protestant's got away from Rome to get away from false doctrine and persecution and for taking a stand for the truth of God's Word, the Bible! It was upon this foundation that America was built...! Martin Luther found 95 instances where Church doctrine was out of line with the Bible! (Likewise in South Africa the Hugenots were Protestants who fled France, Holland and other countries of Europe and laid the foundations upon which South Africa was built.)

Satan's 'truth' has an 'angle of error,' no matter how good it may sound, if it does not align itself completely with the Word of God, then it is not from God – the gap between what is the truth and what Satan would like it to be. Satan does not want us to remain in line with the Word of God. That is his goal.

To explain this we can draw an analogy with rat poison which basically is made up of 99.95% good food and only .05% poison – why would they eat it? – the reason's rat's eat it is because it is the 99.95 % good food that they enjoy, they are unaware of the .05% that kills!

The stronghold of the mind is therefore the strategic centre of the war with the god of this system, because it is primarily through the mind that he holds captives in his power. [13]

The Reformers were prepared to die for their beliefs, not today's Protestant leaders and herein lies the danger. At

---

13   Jesse Pera Lewis. *The Battle of the Mind* p.4

this late hour unless the Protestant world can set aside all it's divisions, all false doctrine and come together in truth as one united body, divided they shall fall. Nothing short of a 'Revival' will change the situation, but in the time that remains is this likely to happen? So, for the individual the Bible counsel in Revelation 18.4...is to ' Get out of her. 'To get out of any form of religion that has any signs or traces of the influence of ….. Satan's false system of worship that the Bible calls Babylon the Great.

And yes, Ecumenism is a spurious and crafty device that is being used to bring Protestantism down and made subject to Rome with the Jesuits overjoyed watching Protestantism as they put it, in it's 'death throes.'

<u>Already the mainline churches have been deceived into going along with Ecumenism in the 'let's all get along' spirit that is put across!</u>

If Satan is to succeed in his efforts to disqualify vast numbers from qualifying for God's Kingdom then clearly the focus in these last days will be on 'swaying' and <u>deceiving the masses.</u>

<u>People are going to be deceived, vast multitudes of them will be deceived into receiving the Mark of the Beast...give them a copy of this</u>

<u>It doesn't matter what percentage of 'rot' is in the system. What matters is that there is a link between the Antichrist and Satan! What matters is that the dragon (Satan) gives the Antichrist his seat, his power and authority. Also that some high ranking individuals are involved.</u>

"Whereof it followeth Rome to be the seat of the antichrist, and the pope to be the very antichrist himself. I

could prove the same by many scriptures, old writers and strong reason!"[14]

"A Great Cloud of Witnesses; Wycliffe, Tyndale, Luther, Calvin, Bunyan, the translator of the King James Version and men who published the Westminster and Baptist Confession of Faith; Sir Isaac Newton, Wesley, Whitfield, Jonathan Edwards and more recently, Spurgeon, Bishop J C Ryle and Dr. Marin Lloyd-James; these men among countless others, all saw the office of the Papacy as the antichrist."[15]

<u>What is happening is that the Roman power is twisting Christianity into giving worship towards the East</u> – again it is heavy on the heart. Rome is calling for all other churches to come together in unity and to acknowledge the Papal primacy.

<u>Sunday is the day we worship, it is our mark of authority.</u> **<u>The Church is above the Bible</u> and the fact that people are bowing down to it is proof of that fact.**

Sunday ….is so called because the day was originally dedicated to the sun, or it's worship. [16]

Sunday (Dies Solis of the Roman calendar, 'day of the Sun,') dedicated to the sun, the first day of the week.[17]

Interestingly <u>Sunday is the title of the Sun God.</u>

"Sabbath…A Hebrew word signifying rest….Sunday was a name given by the heathen to the first day of the week because it was the day on which to worship the Sun."[18]

---

14   Thomas Crammer 1489 – 1546 '*Works of Crammer*, Vol. 1, p. 6-7
15   *All Roads Lead to Rome*, Dorchester House Publishers, Michael de Semelyn, p. 205, 1991.
16   Webster's Dictionary 19th Ed.
17   Schaffer Hergen Encyclopedia . Sunday
18   John Eadle, D.D. LLD …*A Bible Encyclopedia*, p. 561

'The Church took the pagan Sunday and made it the Christian Sunday …. And thus the pagan Sunday, dedicated to Balder, became the Christian Sunday, sacred to Jesus.'[19]

So, who changed it, the Bible or the Church? "Sunday is our mark of authority…The Church is above the Bible and thus transference of Sabbath observance is proof of that fact."

"You may read the Bible from Genesis to Revelation and you will not find a single line authorizing the sanctification of Sunday. The Scriptures infer the religious observance of Saturday."[20]

Here the Catholic system is saying that if you acknowledge Sunday as the day of worship, you are acknowledging the authority of Rome, you are not only acknowledging her as the supreme power, but you are acknowledging that she is above the Bible ….. and Sabbath transference from Saturday to Sunday is proof of that fact. There is no way you can get around it, it is confirmed in their own documentation.

This is what Albert Smith said about Protestants, protesting the removal of the authority of God and the Bible;

"If Protestants would follow the Bible, they would worship God on the Sabbath Day. In keeping the Sunday they are following a law of the Catholic Church.[21]

God is outside this system of worship – that is why His call is 'to come out of her (I'm not in there) This is God's Final Call! The Roman Catholic system has abrogated the laws of God.

---

19   *Catholic World*, March 1894. p 809.
20   James Cardinal Gibbons, *Faith of Our Fathers* p. 89
21   Albert Smith, Chancellor of the Archdiocese of Baltimore, replying for the Cardinal in a letter dated Feb 10, 1920

6. LOOKING INSIDE RELIGION

In all religions there is an Exoteric and an Esoteric sector.[22] Those on the outside, the masses and the few who constitute the inner core or circle. It is the same in Secret Societies where only those at the very centre of the organization are fully informed and aware of what is going on.

So it is with the church where the vast majority are sincere, dedicated God fearing people totally unaware about what is going on deep inside the church and there is much evidence to show that this would apply to most churches today! Details of what is going on in the churches can be found in 'God's Final Call.'

During a 33 degree Freemason initiation ceremony the oath is taken with every Shriner kneeling and taking the oath before the altar with the Qu'ran on top in the name of Allah, thus acknowledging this pagan god of vengeance as his own (the God of our Fathers) And in the reduct, he acknowledges Islam, the declared blood – enemy of Christianity as the one true path. (Who seeketh Islam, earnestly seeks true direction.)

When you become a 33 degree Mason you know you worship Lucifer, **so can we find any of these in Protestantism?**

In the Supreme Temple Architects Hall of Honor one finds paintings of President Harry S Trumann 33 degree. Among the other paintings of outstanding American leaders are also high degree (33 degree) Freemasons who are church leaders, who are these people?

---

22   *Mystical Traditions – Religious Traditions*, Gary H.Kah

- **Dr Norman Vincent Peale**: 33degree - Grand Chaplain of the New York, Knight Templar Shrine.
- **Bishop Carl J Saunders**: 33 degree - Bishop of the United Methodist Church (how can you be Head of the Methodist Church and worship Lucifer?)
- **Rabbi Seymour Atlas**: 32 degree - KCCH
- **Dr James Westerbury**: 32 degree - Ex Director and Editor of Sunday Georgia: Baptist Church
- **Rev Louis R Grant**: - District Sup, The United Methodist Church
- **Rev Billy Graham**: 33 degree - World's most popular 'Protestant' Baptist Evangelist
- **Dr Robert Schuller**: 33 degree - Pastor of the Chrystal Cathedral and host of 'Hour of Prayer' TV program
- **Oral Roberts**: 33 degree - Founder of the Oral Roberts University
- **Jesse Jackson**: 33 degree - Price Hall Freemason

Again, The Reformers were prepared to die for their beliefs, not today's Protestant leaders.

Today, there are a multitude of Bibles, how does one choose? Wherever the so called 'Counter Revolution' started by the Jesuits gained a foothold, the Vernacular version was suppressed and the Bible kept from the laity. So eager were the Jesuits to destroy the authority of the Bible – the 'Paper Pope' of the Protestant's as they contemptuously called it – that they did not refrain from criticizing it's genuiness and historical value to the law and to the testimony.

Scriptures that help identify the truth were gradually put away or hidden.

Over 64,000 words have been removed from the

modern translations in the past 140 years.

No one will enter the New World Order unless he or she will make a pledge to worship Lucifer. No one will enter the New Age unless he will take a Luciferian initiation. The light reveals to us the presence of the Christ comes from Lucifer. He is the light-giver, he is aptly named the 'Morning Star' because it is his light that heralds for man the dawn of a great consciousness.[23]

Well, that is only part of the story, but sufficient to show that there definitely is something going on, without going into how those who refuse to bow down to the beast will be rounded up and how concentration camps are already in existence and ready both in the United States and around the world .....

The true name of Satan, the cabalists say is Yaweh (God) or a reversal of the tetragrammaton – (written in reverse, upside down, pressed together it spells 'Allah')

When the Mason learns that the key to the warrior and the blood is the proper application of the dynamo of living power, he has learned the mystery of his craft. The seething energies of Lucifer are in his hands and before he may step onward and upward he must prove his ability to properly apply them to the enemy.

The Shriner is available to every 32 degree Mason – the 'Shrine Army of Masonry.'

Martin Luther recharged them when he came across a Bible and from it found that what he had been taught was not in line with the Bible. This led to the Reformation, Luther 1483 – 1537, followed by Calvin, John Knox and others.

23   David Spangler, Director of Planetary Initiation, UN www.cuttingedge.org/news

Luther split the angle of error into 95 different concepts and maintained that the Bible was the ultimate authority and that he would do what he had to do to correct matters .

Today the identity of the Antichrist is covered up, but back then they knew and were prepared to die for it.

In 1521 Luther was called to recant before the Church hierarchy he said "I cannot submit my fault either to the Pope or the council, because it is clear as day they have frequently erred and contradicted each other. Unless therefore, I am convinced by the testimony of Scripture...I can and will not retract...Here I stand...I can do no other, So help me God, Amen!"

Directory of the Inquisitors, p 144,148,169 says;

"He who is without the church can neither be reconciled nor saved. He is a heretic; who does not believe what Rome hierarchy teaches – A heretic merits the pains of fire. – By the Gospel, the cannons; civil law and custom, heretics must be burned"

In the millions people were killed as they stood up to the Roman Catholic Church.

Daniel 7.25 reads....*And he (the antichrist) shall wear out the saints of the most high...until a time, and times and dividing of times.*

For 1260 years (from 538AD to 1798 AD) in fulfillment of this prophecy the Papacy tried to destroy Christianity by removing the Bible, by destroying it's people, causing many to flee as was the case of those who boarded the 'Mayflower.' and helped make the United States the 'land of the free.'

But if you can't beat them, join them and this is where the deception comes through;

Speaking of the Papacy, John Wesley wrote, He is in an emphatical sense, the Man of Sin, as he increases all manor of sin above measure. <u>And he is too, properly styled the Son of Perdition, as he caused the death of numberless multitudes, both of his opposes and followers…..</u>'Satanic'

<u>What is the Methodist's position today</u>?

'Methodists To Confirm Catholic Theology On Justification'[24]

<u>The Antichrist is drawing the whole world into Sun Worship – even if the members are not aware of it, this is what Rome is doing.</u>

<u>Ecumenism is the greatest threat to Christianity , it puts Christ on the same level as false Gods.</u>

<u>Jesus is asking us to bow to His authority, not Rome's</u>

All religion is involved in sun worship.

The Pope is the only one to be a world evangelist; he could visit all faiths – Islam and Judaism. <u>He prepared the way for a religious new world order.</u>[25]

RESPECT FOR RELIGION URGENT

In the current International context the Catholic Church remains committed to encourage peace and understanding between peoples and individuals it is necessary and urgent that religion and their symbols be respected.

<u>The tradition of the Dragon and the Sun is echoed in every part of the world.</u> **There was a time when the four points of**

---

24 His Eminence, Sunday Mbong, World Methodist Council (WMC) Chairperson
25 BBC Apr 2, 2005

the world were covered with temples sacred to the Sun and the Dragon: but the cult is now preserved mostly in China and Buddhist countries.

The closer one looks at religion, the more obvious it becomes that the whole world follows the beast, exactly the same things are to be found in them all and all nations have drunk of her wrath.

Again, the call from heaven is …'Come out of her My People.' Revelation 18: 1 – 5

A Compromised view – that God is not Almighty, is the idea most Christian's have. A logical view - a gap theory which attempts to marry evolution with creation by identifying with the antichrist.

By identifying with the antichrist people get involved in cult doctrines that have the agenda to lead people into various forms of sun worship – the Baalhadad, an ongoing process of renewal – the sun is dying and being reborn, which is the core of the reincarnation view – that every time you die you are said to come back to a higher level.

In ancient Egypt we have the 'all seeing eye' within the various forms of sun worship, like the papacy holding up the Eucharist symbol which he puts into the mantra symbolizing the sun inside the crescent moon. By holding up this sun symbol the pope is able to get Christian's to bow down to this form of sun worship, but how does this work in accordance with the agnostic evolution theory?

Who is the Creator of Evolution? According to the Evolutionist it is the Sun.

The Bible says of Jesus - I give light and life. Or you turn to the evolutionists who say it is the sun, which is just another marketing tool used by Lucifer to get agnostics to bow down to him through Sun worship.

The theory that we are somehow evolving to something higher comes from the Jesuits and is displayed on the Vatican's own website.

460. 'For the Son of God became a man so that we might become God... wanting to make us slaves in his divinity, assumed our nature, so that he, made man, might make men gods.'[26] [27]

This is a fulfillment of the lie in Eden....'no you won't die you will become gods.'

<u>The implications of Darwin's theory created a deep divide in culture, a conflict of natural verses supernatural order.</u> **Not only did it offer an alternate account of the Geneses of life of the Old Testament, but it also** <u>gave a sense of moral freedom</u> **from the Divine Creator and His Judgment; ....Darwinism, as the collective theories were called, changed the course of man's history forever. Twofold reasons :-** <u>If Geneses is not accurate, then what about the rest of the Bible</u> also what about one species being more advanced than another?

The Reformers were prepared to die for their beliefs, not today's Protestant leaders.

When Billy Graham retired, Dr James Dobson filled his place. *'Dobson is unrivalled as an evangelical leader, given Billy Graham's advanced age'* said Richard Land, President of the 16 million strong Southern Baptist Convention's Ethics and Religion Liturgy Commission.

---

26   *Catechism of the Catholic Church*, Part 1 (The Professions of Faith
27   *The Profession of the Christian's Faith*, Chapter 2. http://www.vatican.va/archive/catechism/p122a3pl.htm

So it's James Dobson who stepped in to fill the void ... with the 'IHS' on his pulpit, which unknown to most stands for 'Isis, Horus, Set' ... there is no end to the deception, it goes on and on...

What does Billy Graham say about standing up for the truth as a Protestant – let him say it...."there is a difference between fundamentalism and intolerance – I felt that God had called me to love all whether Protestant or Catholic.

So by taking a stand for the Bible was not loving all – <u>that's where the poison comes in.</u> This is where you can identify them by their true colors. <u>You see God loves all by standing on truth, he calls all people into truth and out of error.</u>

See how deceptive it is...work with the Catholics ... we have almost 100% support of Catholic's that was not possible even 20 years ago, we have bishops, archbishops and even the Pope is our friend and we have plans for a couple of events that will probably be world news about our relationship with the Church.

The Jesuits were founded to bring Protestants back to Rome. The high degree Freemasons that were filtered into Protestantism are saying the same things that Billy Graham is saying, that 20 years ago there was almost no interaction with the Catholic Church and today the Pope is our friend and that there are events coming up to show how close we are to the Roman Church – <u>today Protestants are acknowledging Rome as their leader.</u>

<u>These people are getting Christian's involved in liturgy</u> – **where does this come from – this comes from Vatican II, the drive to get Protestants involved in liturgy, not only do they**

get Protestants to not have the true Bible in their hands, but they get the young people to put the Bible down so that they will accept anything that is put in front of them.[28]

What does he stand for – we know that he comes from the Schuller Institute where 33 degree masons infiltrate into Protestantism in order to 'seed' error.

'Today there is a growing interest in the Second Coming, when will it happen?' It is not for you to know the time nor day – when the disciples wanted to talk about prophecy Jesus switched the conversation to evangelism. He wanted them to concentrate on the mission. Speculating on the exact time of Christ's return is futile...only the father knows.

If you want Jesus to come back sooner focus on fulfilling your mission, not figuring out prophecy. [29]

What does the Bible tell us;

<u>Jesus wept over Jerusalem because they were not aware of the hour of their being inspected</u>....**Prophecy is absolutely essential not only in knowing the time, but getting away from deception.**

Both Bill Hybels and Rick Warren have gone so far as to say 'It is critical that we keep in mind a fundamental principle of Christian communication; the audience, (not the message,) is sovereign.... Our message has to be adapted to the needs of the audience. [30]

So it's a 'Man Centered Philosophy: It's people that matter not the message! Figure out what mood you want

---

28   Rick Warren *'The Purpose Driven Church'*, Time Magazine's : THE MAN WITH THE PURPOSE
29   *Purpose Driven Life* p.285, 286
30   *Marketing the Christ* p. 145 Colorado Springs New Press 1988

your sermon to project and then create it! [31]

We made a strategic decision to stop singing hymns in our seeker services.[32]

Saddleback now has a complete pop/rock orchestra.[33]

Use more performed music than congregation singing.[34]

The ground we have in common with unbelievers is not the Bible but our common needs, hurts and interests as human beings. You cannot start with a text. [35]

(So again, notice the deception, it's not the Bible, it is our common needs – put the Bible aside!)

Needs based religion is a most subtle form of pantheism, releasing the god within. I come to church not to hear the Word of God …I come to get my needs served/fulfilled…a bank loan from a buddy or some other need…. he says there is an agenda about going to church.

<u>The Bible says the exact opposite – don't worry about what you need - worry about what the Lord wants. We can't change the Word of God to suite ourselves!</u>

Matthew 6: 31 -33….*take no thought about what you are to eat or what you will wear…..*

32. (for after these things the Gentiles are going) for your Heavenly Father knoweth that ye have need of all these things

33. Seek first the Kingdom.

What about other Protestant Pastors; Well, let's look at Benny Hinn, look at his website, the suits he wears have the

---

31 Ibid p. 269
32 Ibid p. 285
33 Rick Warren – *The Purpose Driven Church*, p. 290
34 Ibid p. 291
35 Ibid p.295

look of Catholicism. He is known to be a Templar - insider of Catholicism – those that spit on the cross.

"Don't say 'I have. Say I Am, I am, I am"

Don't tell me you have Jesus, You are everything he was and everything he shall be[36]

When he puts his hand up - this comes from Mesmer conducting a magnetic séance. Benny waving his hand over a mesmerized subject!

He is an insider infiltrant. The video shows him saying, "Come on here people let me prove the Lord Satan" – a slip of the tongue? Also in the video he sends out a curse on the audience to the effect that any who watch and condemn his ministry be cursed!

What about Kenneth Copeland and wife Gloria

'You have a God in you, you are one' (The Force of love, audio tape 1987)

'Now Peter said by exceeding great and precious promises you become partakers of the divine class. All right, are we god's? We are a class of gods! [37]

Pantheism subtly covered up.

That Adam was God manifest in the flesh 'God's reason for creating Adam was His desire to reproduce Himself....He did just that. He was not a little like God. He was not almost like God. He was not subordinate to God even. Adam is as much like God as you and I could get, just the same as Jesus... Adam in the Garden of Eden, was God manifest in the flesh. Serpent language.[38]

---

36   *Our Pastor in Christ* #2 The Word Made Flesh ....Audiotape, side 2
37   *Praise the Lord* TV Show Feb 5, 1986
38   *Follow the Faith of Abraham*, side1

He speaks about the biggest failure – the biggest failure was God. He lost the top ranking angel, a third of the angels, the whole earth, and the whole of mankind. **Satanic!** On Mark Woodman's DVD's[39] there is a video showing how he blames God for getting drunk on the Holy Spirit.

Kenneth Copeland and the words .. 'I AM'

"And I say this with all respect, so that it won't upset you too bad. But I say it anyway! When I read in the Bible where He says I Am, I just smile and say, 'YES, I AM Too!"

These people are insider Freemason's ...this is Insider Pantheism and it's disgusting! The sad part is that their messages are getting to millions and millions of people who believe this stuff! (Believers Voice of Victory, Broadcast July 9, 1987)

<u>Kenneth Hagen</u>

Word of Faith Magazine, July 1997. Can you believe that he placed the Masonic Obelisk on the front cover, not that many would understand this to be occult symbolism. (power of the Sun God) What is he up to?

Tulsa, Oklahoma is the headquarters of the Oral Roberts and Kenneth Hagen.

Kenneth Hagen and his wife started the Worldwide Rhemer Church whose symbol or emblem is the crown with the cross in it - look underneath. Hagan is a wealthy, wealthy man. On the DVD series you can watch the spectacle of him getting drunk on the Holy Spirit with Kenneth Copeland. He says," this is the first time we've had a full manifestation of that" – (this is not from God, it's demonic!) Kenneth Hagen Blesses ... Kenneth Copeland - ridiculous/pathetic –

---

39   Available from info@Homebase.org

Unbelievable things are happening in this church. Satanic salutes, handshakes and other sublime occult symbolism are openly on display. You would however, need to view the DVD's to get the full impact of these goings on within Christianity.

TV Joshua claims— "I was sent to earth to save the world."

But the Bible says No! Jesus was!

7. MASONRY

If you trace Masonry up through all it's Orders, till you come to the grand tip-top, head Mason of the World, you will discover that the dread individual and the Chief of the Society of Jesus are one and the same person. (he wears black all the time) [40]

The most powerful person in the world some might say is the U.S. President, but the truth is that it is the Jesuit General, Peter Hans Kolvenbach. How do we know that he is more powerful than the Pope, well the book by Nino la Bello explains; The Pope's confessor, an ordinary priest must be a Jesuit; he must visit the Vatican once a week at a fixed time and he alone may absolve the Pope of his sins.[41]

See my lord, from this room – from this room I govern not only Paris, but China: not only China, but the whole world, without any one knowing how I manage.
Michael Angelo Tomburini, 1720 General of the Jesuit's Speaking to Duke of Brancan[42]

President Woodrow Wilson – Some of the biggest men in the United States in the field of commerce and manufacturing are afraid of something. They know that there

---

40   'The Black Pope,' M F Cusack, Middleton, Idaho; CHJ Publishing 1999 p.302.
41   The Vatican Empire, Nino Le Bello, New York: Trident Press, 196 p. 78
42   History of the Jesuit's, Andrew Steinmetz. Philippines, Penn: Lea and Blanchard, 1848 Vol 1 p. 107

is a power somewhere so organized, so subtle, so watchful, so interlocked, so complete, so pervasive that these had better not speak above their breath when they speak in condemnation of it.

Marquis de Lafayette - French Statesman and General who served in the American Continental Army under General George Washington – *It is my opinion that if the liberties of the United States are destroyed, it will be the subtlety of the Roman Catholic Jesuit Priests, for they are the most crafty, dangerous enemies to our religious liberty. They have instigated most of the wars of Europe*

He [the Black Pope] is the power behind the throne and is the real potential head of the hierarchy. The whole machine is under the strictest rules of military discipline.

U.S. Brig Gen. :- Author of the book: Rome's Responsibility for the Assassination of Abraham Lincoln

Jean Baptiste Janssens 1946 – 1964 - Superior General of the Society of Jesuits In Command of:-
- **The Sovereign Military Order of Malta**
- **Scottish – Rite Shriner Freemasonry**
- **The Order of the Illuminati**
- **The Knights of Columbus**
- **The Knights of the Klu Klux Klan**
- **B'Bai B'nith (Jewish Freemasonry)**
- **The Nation of Islam and it's private army (called the Fruits of Islam)The Mafia Commission**

R W Thompson

[The Jesuits] are the deadly enemies of civil and religious

liberty. Nothing that stands in their way can become so sacred as to escape their vengeance [In 1769] <u>During the night preceding the day appointed for the public ceremony of an announcing the abolition of the Jesuit's, [Pope] Clement XIII was suddenly seized with convulsions and died, leaving the act unperformed.</u> **Cosmerin ...records this event in the terse expressive words:** <u>'The Jesuits had poisoned him.</u>

The truth is, the Jesuits of Rome have perfected Masonry to be their most magnificent and effective tool, accomplishing their purposes against Protestants... (the purpose being to bring Protestants back to Rome.) [43]

---

43   *The Grand Design Exposed*, Middleton, Idaho; CHJ Publishing 1999 p.302

8. A WARNING BY THE LATE POPE JOHN PAUL II

But, notice, the words of the late Pope John Paul II who undoubtedly was a humane, honest and reasonable man who will go down in history for his part in bringing down the 'Berlin Wall' precipitating the collapse of the former Soviet Union. But when history is finally written, perhaps what he said as recorded below will even overshadow his part in the downfall Communism.

"<u>We are now standing in the face of the greatest historical confrontation humanity has gone through</u>. **I do not think that wide circles of American Society or wide circles of the Christian community realize fully it. Stop! Read this again!**

We are now facing the final confrontation between Pope John Paul II, the church and the anti – Church of the Gospel verses the anti – Gospel.[44]

Ignoring the second part of his message **we need to realize that something is going to happen, something of enormous importance!** Was the Pope trying to sound a warning to American's, in fact to all American's regardless of denomination? If not, why the use of the words 'wide circles of America Society or the Christian Community' in almost <u>cryptic language</u> and why would this be on his personal website and not the Vatican's. Also, why was it not simply addressed to the faithful, his flock?

The great man that he was, undoubtedly knew what

---

44   Cardinal Karol Wojtyla (Pope John Paul II) http:///www.indarticles.com/articles/ml_mOMKY/ls_9_27/al_108881880

was afoot and likely strongly disapproved and wanted desperately to warn people, all people, especially those in America, hoping that they will wake up before it was too late! Obviously, he could say no more, not wanting to suffer a fate similar to that of Pope Clement XIII who was poisoned on the eve of his announcing the disbandment of the Jesuits.

'Anybody who is acquainted with the state of affairs in the Vatican in the last 35 years is well aware that the prince of darkness has had and still has his accomplices in the court of St. Peter in Rome.'[45]

"The devil in the Catholic Church is so protected now that he is like an animal protected by the government." Cardinal. Milinge cited papal statements to back up his claims.

No doubt Pope John Paul II was only too well aware of the need to 'watch his back' in those quarters, regardless of his high position!

This is for thinking people everywhere. Writing about this should not be seen as an attack on the church or any ones particular religion, it is done simply to show folk how according to Scripture, the entire world has been deceived by Satan and what to do to ensure your survival. The call from heaven in Revelation 18.4 is *"Come out of her,* **My People."** Like "I'm not in there." **If your system of worship is not warning you of the grave consequences of accepting the Mark of the Beast, then you are in the wrong religion and need to heed the Bibles call to 'Come out of her.'**

But, will people heed this call? These ones need to realize that they were God's People, long before they ever became part of the Church of Rome! As such they are also

---

45 *The Fatima Crusader*, Fr. Malachi Martin

the ones God affectionately calls 'My People.' And it is to Him that their obedience belongs and it is for a protection!

Hopefully, the foregoing will provide food for thought that will lead to positive thinking and action, as all too often in history, it is only afterwards that men will admit that they might have done more to avert some otherwise needless tragedy, for when good men fail to act, 'Evil Triumphs.' That is the message of this book that surely both Pope John Paul II and Mark Woodman would want conveyed to the world!

9. SATAN'S RIGGED SYSTEM – THE SECULAR WORLD THAT IS RUINING THE EARTH

Can it be denied that there is a huge problem facing the world's freedom loving people with no easy or simple solution in sight, save turning to the one and only source of true wisdom? Proverbs 1.33 explains...*the one listening to me.... Will reside in security and be undisturbed from dread of calamity.* But, for most because of stubborn pride, that will only be a last resort. Dare we continue in this way with our leaders knowingly or unknowingly serving or being used by Satan?

Can we continue to ignore our Maker? Surely it would make more sense to at least pause and think again about where we are and ask why? Perhaps a good way to start the process would be by revisiting who God is, although this would be the last thing the world would want us to do. Rarely if ever does He even get a mention in our now almost totally secular world. But, if that were somehow to change, the freedoms that would follow are simply too mind boggling to even imagine.

In your minds eye, picture moths and insects flying around a bright light burning themselves out in a senseless frenzy? Does that not fittingly describe Satan's system, our world today, the phony, rigged system that we find ourselves in, with all its grand illusions, its graft and deceit, designed to control the world's population?

What is going on is really all about control, the ultimate form of control, **a global fascist state. Like lambs we are** being led to the slaughter by the imposition of a World order government. The Illuminati and those behind it are seeking to impose their will on humanity at the instigation of the one behind them, who since Eden has been <u>trying to impose his will on all humanity</u> in defiance of God!** Conspiracy author David Icke, although not professing any religious beliefs, explains the many ways that this is being carried out in his book 'Children of the Matrix.' He notes Henry Ford saying that "people of this nation do not understand our banking and monetary system, for if they did, I believe there would be a revolution before tomorrow evening."

There is no aspect of our lives that is not being controlled when the real facts are examined. Even the water we drink is contaminated, anything made from fluoridated water, including beer and soft drinks is effected. They're not only dumping toxic fluoride into our drinking water, but along with it are fluoride additives containing deadly carcinogenic elements, lead, arsenic and radium. Fluorinated water was first used in Nazi prison camps. German scientists found that fluoride causes various mental disturbances, makes people stupid, docile, subservient and allows for mass control. It also shortens lives and damages bone structure. However, telling the whole story about how behind the scene, our entire system is being rigidly controlled, would fill volumes.

We don't need this, we need to move away from Satan's false light and away from his false promises, and look up and see the vast expanse of real creation and know that there is a God, a Mighty God of Creation, not this fallen rebellious angel and impostor who cannot create and is so intent upon our destruction and blinding us to the truth about God. <u>But,</u>

<u>being blessed with free will, not until we call upon Him (and this is key), can God and will God act to free us from our present bondage, his hands are tied. We are the ones who must decide whom we wish to serve.</u>

In this war about worship, what needs to be realized is that God is both the source and the supreme example of love. God is love I John 4.8. We have neither seen God nor heard his voice. Yet he invites us to enter into a loving relationship with him. How can we do that? The first step to toward loving anyone is to take in knowledge of that one. We cannot feel deep affection for someone we do not know. So he has provided his Word, the Bible, so that we can learn about him. He wants us to know everything about him and his creation. He has given us the privilege of prayer…James 4.8 tells us….*Draw close to God and he will draw close to you.* He is our Heavenly Father who wants only the very best for each one of us. He is patient and kind, long suffering and good, but that is not the image Satan wants us to have of him. Instead he wants us to see God in the worst possible light, as revengeful, hateful and the cause of our suffering.

We were created in God's image, we were given his just laws and commandments, we were designed to love. He wants us to serve him because we love and desire his righteous way of ruling. Love is essential for the peace and harmony of all creation. We were not designed for a mere three score and ten years, he put eternity in our hearts. Ecclesiastes 3.11. It was through Satan that death entered the world and that is the only thing he wants for us……he has deceived the whole world and it is time for that to stop!

So great was God's love that He was even prepared to

offer up his Son so that all might have everlasting life. Is it not reasonable that our perfect Heavenly Father would expect us to show loving appreciation for all he has done for us? But there are limits even to his patience and certainly he will act soon to restore his creation to righteousness and bring an end to *those ruining the earth* Revelation 11.18. He will not allow Satan's world, with it's 'might is right', 'winner takes all,' 'survival of the fittest' system of selfishness, violence and greed to continue a day longer than justice requires.

No matter what may come we can always find solace, comfort and refuge in the book of Psalms; Ps 23, Ps 121, Ps 37. Ps.80.

This information is for freedom loving people everywhere, especially the American people. **Once America 'Get's It' so too will the world and the world will be a better place**. Otherwise it will continue to spiral down into death and destruction.....But your help is needed, please don't keep this vital information to yourself, share it with family and friends and may God Bless your efforts.

10. A WAR ABOUT WORSHIP

Another very important reason for writing this book is to awaken and rekindle belief in the human spirit, for again 'when good men fail to act, evil triumphs.' All that it would take to put an end to this sheer and utter insanity is for a few good men to understand what is going on and to stand up and say, "Enough" and take whatever steps necessary to close down his operation, the cover that the church provides. Once exposed for what it really is, the entire charade will be over, for nothing can justify what is going on! However, Satan's gamble is that this will not happen and that few would even dare mention this and as such, that his intimidation tactics will work. Oh! that he may be proved wrong.

May a scripture found in 2 Kings 6:16 provide encouragement for us to stand firm...*Do not be afraid, for there are more with us than who are against us.* Elisha prayed and his servant's eyes were opened to see......*the mountainous region was full of horses and chariots of fire all around...Angelic hosts.* Far greater in number than the Syrian Kings military force and this is true today, God and many myriads of mighty angels are posed and ready to go into action to remove wickedness from the world!

So with that assurance, the first thing we need to do is free ourselves. We need to let go of the fear of what other people think of us for standing up for the truth. We need to free ourselves from being followers and step out of the herd mentality and to stop rushing to stop others from trying to escape the insanity of the present system. When we do that we will cease to be the sheepdogs keeping others in line. We will respect the uniqueness of others and allow them the freedom of thought and expression. We will lead and others will follow. We will stand up and play our part in changing the world from a prison to a paradise in the knowledge that God helps those who help themselves!

Hopefully, what this book will also accomplish will be, a 'Revival of Faith' and of true Christian Unity and a move away from false religion to bring a resounding shout of Praise to God and His Holy Name, so that He may act to 'lessen or cut short those days,' the days of the coming Great Tribulation and <u>show people that unless they start paying attention that they will be bringing all this tribulation upon themselves!</u>

What the people also need to realize, which comes across in <u>Deuteronomy Chapter 28</u> is that <u>we are now in the time of the Biblical Maledictions or curses</u> and that as recipients of the 'birthright blessings,' that those blessings have come and gone with little or no appreciation. Can it be denied that ever since 9/11 there has been a decided change for the worse in America's fortunes as God removes himself as comes across in Hosea 5.15...*I shall go, I will return to my place until they bear their guilt and they will certainly seek my face! When they are in sore straits, they will seek me!*

The most critical issue facing the American people in this time of moral degeneration and ungodliness, is how to prevent America's God given sovereignty and freedom from being surrendered or exchanged for a Fascist World Government under the United Nations that will bring great tribulations not only to America but the entire world?

Certainly by virtue of it's people having *free will* this is something only they can decide. However, it is likely that the majority would even welcome a World Order Government as a monumental event in world history, unless they can be told the truth and about what is really going on and what lies ahead. Unfortunately, that is where they are now in Satan's system. **But they need to realize that if this is allowed to happen and that if a World Order Government is established, God will have no part in it and will remove himself as indicated in Hosea 5.15 and America will find herself on her own without the Divine Hand of Protection and will be totally exposed to Satanic machinations. Thus the urgent need for the 'Seek Him Early ' message to get out!**

Certainly getting rid of God's people Israel has always been Satan's number one priority. He has tried and failed in two World Wars and is now engaged in 'softening' them up with a literal barrage of satanic propaganda to create a 'freedom from care' attitude designed to take them off guard, before his third and final attempt to bring them down.

11. GOD'S PEOPLE ISRAEL

Reference to 'God's people Israel' should not be confused with today's modern state of Israel, but rather to **the Anglo-American people who today constitute the main body of the 'Lost tribes of Israel'** mentioned in the Bible. In fact the very first instruction Jesus gave his disciples was ...to *go continually to the lost sheep of the house of Israel*....Matthew 10.6., indicating the importance Jesus ascribed to this.

Is it not strange that today, while it is readily accepted that the Islamic people are the descendents of Abraham's son Ishmael, the identity of the descendents of Abraham's other son Isaac, is not so readily accepted or even known.

In Geneses 22.17 it was foretold that Jacob's descendents would be......*multiplied like the stars of the heavens and grains on the seashore* and according to Geneses 27.28. they would be given the *...choicest and most fertile parts of the earth...*(not a mere strip of land along the coast of Palestine occupied by today's modern state of Israel!)

A short version of the story about the 'lost tribes of Israel' would be that after the collapse of the Assyrian Empire around 612 B.C. the Northern ten tribe kingdom of Israel disappeared into history and became known as the 'ten lost tribes of Israel.' What is not known about them and has somehow become obscured by history or kept hidden is that they gradually migrated into and across Europe in two great waves. In the first wave they were known to historians as the Cimmerians – or Celts and later, in a second wave they were known as the Scythian or Sacae tribes (sons of Sac – Isaac.)

Also, that after a withholding period of seven Biblical times (2520 years) from the time of their Assyrian captivity around 721 B.C., with incredible suddenness they or more specifically the dual thirteenth tribes of Ephraim and Manasseh (sons of Israel's youngest and favorite son Joseph – see Geneses Chapter 48 also 1 Chronicles 5.1 and 2 which clearly states that …. **right of first born was given to the sons of Joseph.** (A key Scripture to Bible understanding that seems to have been missed by Bible students) would suddenly emerge on to the world scene as the Anglo-American dual world power and would be recipients of the 'birthright promises' of unprecedented national wealth and power. Interestingly, 2520 years later in 1800 A.D. the Federal Government moved from Philadelphia, Pennsylvania to the new Capital of the United States in Washington D.C. Certainly the other tribes were also blessed, but not to the same extent as Ephraim and Manasseh, again a brief account of this can be found in Genesis chapter 49.

Notice Isaiah 45.19...*In a dark place...I spoke not; nor said I to the seed of Jacob, "Seek me simply for nothing.' 49. "You are my servant, O' Israel, you the one in whom I shall show my beauty."* **Deuteronomy 28.2 ...If you are careful to do all I am commanding you....your God will put you high above all other nations.**

11. You will overflow with prosperity…..

15. if you will not take care to keep his statutes all these maledictions must overtake you….

25 …..you will be defeated before your enemies.

43...the alien resident will keep ascending higher and higher and you lower and lower.

44. He will become head and you tail. While few would be willing to admit it, can it be denied that this is what is happening today?

Notice Psalm 104 verse 42....*For he remembered his holy promise to his servant Abraham.*

43. So he brought out his people (from Egypt) with exultation. Notice God's purpose;

44. And gradually he gave them the lands of the nations...(the choicest and most fertile parts of the earth- unprecedented blessings of wealth and power Deut 28 1-15)

45. To the end that they might keep his regulations and observe his laws.

Notice Exodus 19.5...*if you will strictly obey my voice and keep my covenants, then you will certainly become a special property, because the whole earth belongs to me.*

6. You will become a kingdom of priests and a holy nation.

KEY TO UNDERSTANDING GOD'S PURPOSE FOR HIS PEOPLE ISRAEL (FOR US TODAY) IS THAT; God wanted His Chosen people Israel to become a nation of righteous, God fearing people who would be a <u>living example to people of all nations</u>, showing that God's way's are infinitely better than Satan's and to help free them (the nations) from the chains of Satan's dismal prison with all it's violence, strife, poverty and greed, to the end that all people would learn and benefit from following God's righteous ways. But because of Israel's failure,(and later our failure) Paul was tasked with these responsibilities and made an Apostle to the Nations. When God ...*turned his attention to the people of the nations to take out a people for his name- a spiritual*

Israel. Acts 15.14. But this did not in any way undo God's irrevocable covenant with Abraham and his seed according to their generations to time indefinite. Genesis 17.7

Might it be said that God has always been welcomed into the trenches, but is soon forgotten once peace and prosperity returns and after World War II, that was soon to happen. Instead of becoming a living example to the world of a righteous, God fearing people there was a gradual spiralling down and a lowering of standards in America and countries of the former Allies, which provided the wicked one with the opportunity he needed to bring about our destruction- we have played right into his hands……that is where we are today!

This trend also found it's way into the Protestant churches, where they dropped or relaxed their guard and failed to cherish their Protestant roots and heritage, providing the 'wicked one' with the opportunity to take advantage of the situation to strengthen the hand of Rome in order to achieve his own purposes.

Since the Reformation Protestantism, despite having the Bible gradually became divided into thousands of different sects and denominations each with it's own particular version of the truth, whereas the Roman Catholic Church apart from the Eastern Orthodox Church remained intact. Might it be that divided we have fallen?

In Deuteronomy 31.29 Moses warned….."*For I well know that after my death …you will certainly turn aside from the way I have commanded you;* **and calamity will be bound to befall you at the close of the days** *because you will do what is bad in the eyes of your God so as to offend him by the* *works of your hands."* Like America acting as 'law enforcer' for the Roman Catholic Church and the United Nations!

12. ISRAEL AND THE NATIONS

In the euphoria of victory after WWII the Church was given a free-pass in the Nuremburg Trials for it's role in supporting Hitler in coming into power in Nazi Germany in his Satanic quest to destroy God's people. For the Church saw in Hitler, through Hitler's Vice-Chancellor Baron Von Papen, a 'good Catholic,' the opportunity for the re-establishment of the Holy Roman Empire!

It has always been Israel and the nations, and it would seem that Israel was purposely 'lost' for it's own protection. But now in the present 'let's all get along' world, it would appear that our once great nations are about to cast aside forever, their former glory and throw in their lot with conniving, squabbling, godless politicians that make up the United Nations, with the added prospect of even being relegated to an increasingly subordinate position within the world body or even being ganged up against and removed by the group of ' ten' mentioned in Revelation 17.12 ....who have *as yet not received ' power and authority' as kings....?*

Notice how Revelation 17.16 tells how this 'group of ten' will close down the Great Church, but not before they 'receive authority as kings'.....*and the ten horns that you saw and the wild beast (Satan) these will hate the harlot and will make her devastated and naked and will ...... completely burn her with fire...*

18. The woman whom you saw means the great city that has a kingdom over the kings of the earth. (the Vatican.)

Notice also Satan's position in the matter which clearly indicates that he has only been using the church. Thus the need for the faithful to heed the call in Revelation 18.2,4 tO *'Come out of her....'*

This will not be the first time that the Church will be closed down ....it has happened before during the time of Napoleon when; ..... *'The aged Pontiff was carried off into exile to Valence. The enemies of the church rejoiced. The last Pope they declared had resigned.'* - Church History, p. 24

In 1798 A.D., he (Berthier)...made his entrance into Rome, ABOLISHING THE PAPAL GOVERNMENT AND ESTABLISHED A SECULAR ONE.[46]

Bertheir entered Rome on 10th February, 1798 and proclaimed a Republic. Half of Europe thought Napoleon's veto would be obeyed and that with it the papacy was dead. But in 1929 Mussolini and Cardinal Gasppari signed the Italian Vatican Pact. In terms of the agreement the pope received 750 million Lire for his support of the fascist party. 'The Roman question tonight was a thing of the past and the Vatican was at peace with Italy'....In appending the autographs to this memorable document extreme cordiality was displayed on both sides.[47]

Does it not make sense for our leaders to seriously rethink the entire issue, which to say the least is pitifully full of holes in much of its thinking? Why should this be, is it not **an 'error of judgment' of gigantic proportions** simply because the 'Holy Writings' have been ignored, if only to please the Bishop of Rome and his unseen controller, the Biblical Arch Deceiver? Also, should a New World Order government be <u>fashioned using</u> the European Union and as a model which

46   The Encyclopedia Anniversary 1941 ed.
47   *San Francisco Chronicle* Feb 11, 1929

seems to be what is on the cards? When it seems to be experiencing so much difficulty managing its own affairs, let alone those of the entire world?

We are not living in ordinary times, has America since 9/11 not been on a 'roller coaster' ride down? Have enough mistakes not already been made? If now is not the time to turn matters around by making a stand for truth and righteousness, will that time ever come?

13. THE MALEDICTION'S

What the American people and the world needs to realize, that comes across in Deuteronomy Chapter 28 is that we are now in the time of the Maledictions or curses and that as recipients of the 'birthright blessings,' that the blessings have come and gone with little or no appreciation. Can it be denied that ever since 9/11 there has been a decided change in America's fortunes as God removes himself as comes across in Hosea 5.15...*I shall go, I will return to my place until they bear their guilt and they will certainly seek my face! When they are in sore straits, they will seek me!*

The most critical issue facing the American people in this time of moral degeneration and ungodliness, is how to prevent America's God given sovereignty and freedom from being surrendered or exchanged for a World Government under the United Nations that will only bring great tribulation?

Certainly by virtue of it's people having *free will* this is something only they can decide. However, it is likely that the majority would even welcome a World Government as a monumental event, in world history unless they can be told what is actually going on and what really lies ahead for them. Unfortunately, this is where they are now in Satan's system.

But they need to realize that if this is allowed to happen, **God will have no part in it and will remove himself as indicated in Hosea 5.15 and America will find itself on her own without the Divine Hand of Protection and will be totally exposed to Satanic machinations. Thus there is an urgent need for the 'Seek Him Early ' message to get out!**

Certainly getting rid of God's people Israel remains Satan's first and number one priority. He has tried and failed in two World Wars and is now engaged in 'softening' them up with a literal barrage of satanic propaganda to create a 'freedom from care' attitude designed to take them off guard, before his third and final attempt to bring them down.

While on the subject of the Maledictions notice Deutoronomy 28.23 *Your skies will become copper and the earth beneath your feet iron*

24. God will give powder and dust as rain!

Might this be the real cause of 'global warming and climate change' that seems to have been missed even by the clergy whose God given responsibility it is to be knowledgeable about such matters and to keep us properly informed!

14. THE WORLD'S GREATEST SCAM

It would seem that the leadership and elite of the entire world have been corrupted into thinking that somehow they will be the Masters and the rest of us slaves or mind controlled robots in the coming World Order government or dictatorship and that they have bought into with all the Satanic lies and deception, <u>not realizing that in the process, unbeknown even to themselves that they are also being deceived and are simply being used by him to achieve his purposes, which is the destruction of humanity of which they are a part!</u> He is the Arch Deceiver?

But what also seems to escape these ones is that the world's first religion was 'Narsiscism' and that it was Satan who introduced it, his 'I Am' philosophy, that us mortals somehow are god's or evolving into a godhead that is freely expounded in our centres of higher education. It is this that he has used so successfully to deceive so many and to deny the very existence of Almighty God! Again, should he be trusted? <u>What guarantees have been secured for surrendering the sovereignty of the United States?</u>

Certainly the Bible tells that there definitely will be a world government, but shows that America and its great resources will only being used to put it in place, after which it's rulership will pass to …. *ten kings who have not yet received a kingdom…*Revelation 17.11-13. How can this not be seen as perhaps the World's Greatest Deception or Scam? [But, if those days were to be 'lessened' none of the above might even be necessary. Does that not provide us the hope, the chance that we so desperately need?]

Beyond the call for a New World Religion, a 'Cosmic Christ' and all the other New Age 'think,' when all is said and done, what this is really all about comes across in **Psalm 83.4...'***Let us efface them from being a nation, that the name of Israel may be remembered no more.'* That has always been the wicked ones goal. Satan will not relent until that has happened, <u>that is what this is all about!</u>

Now with God in the process of removing himself as comes across in Hosea 5.15 and with the Great Tribulation and the Maledictions straight ahead. <u>We of our own volition, will soon find ourselves completely on our own and totally exposed, without that Divine Hand of Protection, in an increasingly dangerous world!</u>

Before leaving the Book of Genesis we note that Abraham had a son Ishmael and likewise Jacob had a son Esau, but neither of these was to inherit the birthright promises. A brief account of this follows; Regarding Hagar's son, Ishmael... in Genesis 16.1 we read ...Sarai, (Sarah) Abram's (Abraham) wife, had borne him no children, but she had an Egyptian maidservant and her name was Hagar.

3. The Sarah...gave her to Abram.

4...she became pregnant (by Abram).

6...Then Sarah began to humiliate her...so she ran away.

7...**Later God's angel found her...**

9..."return to your mistress and humble yourself". 10. then God's angel said to her: "I shall greatly multiply your seed"...

11...you shall give birth to a son and must call his name Ishmael. -[Father of the Arab Nations.]

12..As for him, he will become a Zebra of a man. His

hand will be against everyone and everyone's hand will be against him; and before the face of his brothers he will tabernacle.

After the death of Mohammed in 632 A.D. the Arabs had carried the Sword of Islam from the Atlantic to the Indian Ocean, occupying the lands of Spain, Southern France, Sicily, North Africa, Egypt, Arabia, the Holy Land, Armenia, Persia and Afghanistan. The empire of the Arabs was larger than that of Alexander the Great and Rome and for 500 hundred years it carried the torch of civilization. **In Genesis 17.19-21 we read….'I will make you a great nation (Ishmael) but my Covenant I will establish with Israel.'** In time Abraham was to have other children, but at Genesis 25.5…we note…'Abraham gave everything he had to Isaac.' Genesis Chapter 25 gives an account of how Jacob's son Esau lost the birthright.

21. Rebekah (Isaac's wife) became pregnant.

22. And the sons within her began to struggle (Esau and Jacob).

23…God said to her, **"Two nations are in your belly… (two distinct races, a white child and a red one-Caucasian and Arabic, in one womb - a supernatural manipulation?) and the one national group will be stronger than the other, the older will serve the younger.**

30… Jacob said; "Sell me…your right of firstborn.'

32…Esau and of what benefit to me is a birthright.

33…he proceeded to sell his right as first born to Jacob.

34. So Esau despised the birthright

At Hebrews 12.16 we read…'that there may be no one not appreciating sacred things like Esau who in exchange for a meal gave away his rights as firstborn.'

Notice the outcome in Genesis 27.30...as soon as Isaac had blessed Jacob...Esau came back from hunting.

31...Esau said to his father "is there just one blessing you have for me?

39...So Isaac said "Behold away from the fertile soils of the earth your dwelling will be...away from the dew of the heavens"...

40. "And by the sword you will live, and your brother you will serve. <u>But it will occur that when you grow restless, you will indeed *Break His Yoke* off your neck</u>". Is this not something modern day Israel should take heed?

Indeed it is this warning that needs to be taken very seriously when seen against the world's present geopolitical landscape for only recently was it announced that Iran's Mohamud Ahmadinejad had appointed the head of Iran's Revolutionary Guard, Roston Ghasami as the country's oil minister which means he will also be the head of Opec. This year (2011) is Iran's turn to hold the rotating presidential office of Opec. His appointment is seen by many analysts as an indication that Iran could wage economic warfare against the United States and Israel and obviously that this development would pose a major threat to the economy of the free world which is already on the brink of a double dip recession following the down grading of America's credit rating and with the world economy being so heavily dependent upon the free flow of oil. Also despite the recent democratizing efforts in the Arab world, it is still very much divided.

Satan knows that once God has removed himself that

he will be free to bring in his bands to finally destroy God's people Israel as foretold in **Daniel 11.40.....in the time of the end....*the king of the north will storm in with chariots and with horsemen and with many ships*....** Notice how this is described in **Ezekiel 38.. 16....*you will be bound to come up against my people Israel, like clouds to cover the land. In the final part of the days it will occur**

18. And it must occur in that day when Gog comes in upon the soil of Israel....that my rage will come up into my nose.

19. And in my ardor, in the fire of my fury, I shall have to speak.

23 And I shall certainly magnify myself and make myself known before the eyes of many nations ; and they will have to know that I am Jehovah.

In Daniel 12. 1 we notice also....*during that time Michael (Jesus) will stand up, the great prince....there will be a time of great distress* ...**And during that time your people will escape, everyone who is found written down in the book.**

5. As for you O Daniel seal up the book until the time of the end. Many will rove about and true knowledge will become abundant.

So, certain these are the chilling facts and details about what according to the Bible will soon confront humanity.

15. TWO VITALLY IMPORTANT SCRIPTURES

As an individual ones decision will be either to go with the flow and 'take the broad and easy road leading off into destruction' as recorded in Matthew 7.13 or to 'choose the endless life that God has promised.' If there is nothing that you would wish to take from this writing, please try to understand two scriptures, for your very eternity may depend upon it.)

The following two scriptures provide a warning that it would be foolish to ignore; The first is found in Revelation 14. 9... 'If anyone worships the wild beast or it's image (the World Order Government under the U.N.,) and receives a mark.

10. he will also drink the cup of God's wrath.

The other scripture is found in Revelation chapter 17. 8 'those who dwell upon the earth will wonder admiringly, but their names have not been written upon the scroll of life...'

So clearly, bowing down to Satan's World Order Government will ultimately bring about ones destruction at Armageddon.

While Satan has his mark so to does God. According to Ezekiel 9. 3 – 7. In verse we read that ......

4....'those sighing and groaning' over all the detestable things happening would be marked. This is Scripture that you would be encouraged to carefully consider as it provides a glimpse of what will transpire at Armageddon.

Surely it is time to regain some focus and see what is

really going on! Is it not also time for our leaders, those at or close to the top of the pyramid, those who sincerely believe that their involvement up until now has been in the belief that what they are doing will be for the good of mankind, to say, "what have we become part of, we are better than this, we've always been better than this." "How did we allow ourselves to fall so badly, to be so thoroughly duped?"...... <u>and will do whatever is right and in the best interests of the people they are sworn to protect and defend,</u> before it is too late!

What is going on really is a 'no win' situation for Satan and his crowd. He has tried and failed in everything that he has thrown at God and is going to fail in this his last shot when he and his demonic forces will be brought down at Armageddon, but at what cost, that is the real tragedy of the matter. However, it is only after wars that such sentiments are expressed. What is going on really is so totally unnecessary, so needless. But, how can people be made to understand that God has to act to restore order and remove the disorderly and that it is only his people's senseless, stubbornness that is standing in the way, will they understand before it is too late?

16. A WORLD ORDER GOVERNMENT

The idea of a World Order should be relegated back to what it was, just the 'pipe dreams' and good intentions of some 'good old boys' of yesteryear...Morgan, Macy, Rockefeller and all the others not to mention Cecil Rhodes, the Rothchilds and is totally 'out of whack' with the geopolitical realities of today's rapidly changing world order!

Even in his time Churchill recognized this.....'*The United Nations Organization was still very young, but already it was clear that its defects might prove grave enough to vitiate the purpose for which it was created.*' So, we most certainly have been warned.

Alasdair MacIntyre said...."*the religion of the English ...is that there is no god, and it is wise to pray to him from time to time.*" So at least they will know where to go when the going gets tough!

O that you British people might revisit the 'Tilbury Speech' and the words of your beloved and brave queen, Elizabeth I, who spoke from the heart and see again who you are, your roots and how far you have come and realize who it was that made the' *winds blow'.* A thanksgiving service was held in St. Paul's Cathedral for the deliverance of the country and a medal struck with the words *"God blew and they were scattered."(And scattered from Armada's fleet)*

The Queen's confidence in God and her people was rewarded. It was this that made it possible for Britain to avoid becoming subjects of Phillip II of Spain and the Spanish Catholic Empire and instead to go on to become the world's greatest Nation, the Biblical 'Chief of the Nations' (Jeremiah 31.7) with an Empire upon which the sun never sets and to spread abroad the knowledge and truth of Almighty God!

Also, the thirteen British colonies that later became the New England States was the cornerstone uopn which the United States was built.

God's promise to Abraham [of both spiritual and material blessings] was that "in you all the families of the earth shall be blessed."

C.H.Spurgeon in *Treasury of the Old Testament* wrote "*I judge that God has blessed the two great nations of the Anglo-Saxon race-England and the United States - and given them preeminence [so that]...they may spread abroad the knowledge of the Glory of God.*"

How was this tremendous wealth and power? To bring its enemies into submission? No, through the generosity and character of their people's, Europe was rebuilt through the Marshall Plan and likewise the Japan was reconstructed allowing both Germany and Japan to become global economic powers.

James Morris in his work *Pax Britannica* wrote..*'It was not merely the right of the British to rule, so the imperialists thought, it was their duty. They were called.'* **They would distribute across the earth their own methods, principles and liberal traditions that the future of mankind would be reshaped. Justice would be established, miseries relieved.**

At the end of World War II, the United States was to become the most powerful nation on earth in the *'Rise and Fall of Great Powers' by Paul Kennedy* we read: 'America alone, held the secret of the atomic bomb. It also held two-thirds of the world's gold reserves, half its manufacturing production capacity and half its ships and supplied one third of the globe's exports.'

So come on America and you British cousins, clearly it's time to sort this matter out. This is not about creating panic, wild hysteria, doom and gloom, but rather a time for cool heads to accept the realities and truth of the situation and to work towards resolving the matter in a calm and rationale way. This should be a call to both the American people and the British peoples to see again the need to jealously guard your *Freedom and Liberties* in an increasingly dangerous world. **A world that has consistently sought to destroy you and your very existence and where your survival has only been possible through the Divine hand of Providence which you are now in the process of casting aside in exchange for a World Order government under the Church of Rome and the United Nations that will provide Satan, Lucifer or whoever you wish to call him, the world dictatorship he seeks! Surely, this is obvious!**

This should be a call to the American people to jealously guard their *Freedom and Liberty* and to understand the need to properly secure America's Sovereignty by safe- guarding the Bill of Rights, in the knowledge that the federalism created by the U.S. Constitution is flawed and is identical to the federalism of the Grand Lodge system of Masonic government and not the supposed friend of the people but rather their controller.

A perfect example would be when John Marshall the first Chief Justice revealed the Mason's contempt for the people in his denunciation of "Judical review," which simply meant that the Supreme Court was the true power. <u>Where are the checks and balance on the Supreme Court?</u> This becomes particularly clear when considering the make up of the Courts present membership![48]

Also, notwithstanding this, **'WE THE PEOPLE'** - people of the individual states need to be reminded of our (their) power to embrace the 'states rights' under the Constitution and <u>to send to Congress only those who truly understand and support the rights of the people they represent!</u> Those with the necessary resolve and tenacity to work towards the repeal of treaties and agreements that do not truly represent the will of the people that have resulted in millions of jobs being shipped abroad and have brought America closer to a World Government. NAFTA, GATT and all the others. Also, that these elected representatives will work to ensure that the sovereignty and security of individual States are in no way compromised.

---

48   Extracts taken from 'Our Masonic Constitution' http://www.Rense.com

17. CLIMATE CHANGE HIJACKED?

How many Americans are aware that the supposedly good intentioned treaty on 'Climate Change' proposed at the 2009 United Nations Climate Change Conference actually stated in it's 209 page wording that a world government was going to be created. The word government actually appeared as the first of three purposes of the new entity. If the treaty had been signed, legally it would have taken precedence over the Constitution. If the President had signed the treaty it would have been the end of your freedom, democracy and prosperity forever- that is how close it came and obviously this provides a clear indication of how impatient its sponsors are becoming to put a World Government in place and also how ready they are! —

This was Part of A Warning To America by Lord Monckton, a former adviser to Lady Margaret Thatcher who spoke at Bethel University in St. Paul, MN (10/4/09) on the UN Climate Change Treaty that was scheduled to be signed in December 2009. Lord Monckton was hosted by the Minnesota Free Market Institute. (Text thanks to Gary Jacobucci)

Will the 2011 Climate Change Conference succeed in bringing about the World Order Government, where the others failed? We shall soon find out!

At a recent gathering of business leaders in Sandton, Johannesburg as a prelude to the Cope 17 Convention on Climate Change, might the question have been put to the panel which included former American Vice President Al Gore, whether Cope 17 would have anything to do with the implementation of a World Order Government as a former adviser to former British Prime Margaret Thatcher had contended as regards the previous Conference on Climate Change held in Copenhagen? Likely even the most courageous reporter would not have risked putting his job on the line by posing such a question even if he was aware of it.

So, clearly at this eleventh hour there is a real and urgent need for people to start paying very close attention to what is being signed into law, especially international treaty agreements and for experts in such matters to act as watchdogs and do everything within their power to explain and educate the American people about the real threats to their freedom and liberty, in the simplest and most easily understandable language as possible, no matter what it takes.

Need America be reminded that only one of the 45 Declared Communist Goals written into the Congressional record on January 10th 1963 remains to be achieved, a World Government under the United Nations that will be totally fascist in nature, no elections, no democracy, voting, or rights.

The ultimate dictatorship that will put into immediate effect the plan to reduce the world's population to the 5 billion level, and you know what that will mean for the world's Christians, those that will not accept the 'Mark of the Beast'. [49]

---

[49] www.Rense.com

18. THE UN - A PROVISIONAL ENTITY!

Again, how many people realize that the United Nations is actually a provisional entity and that after the Second World War if a peace treaty between Germany and the Allies (which as yet still has not been signed), had been signed, that the UN Charter or mandate would legally have ended?

How many people know that the present German government is in fact illegitimate? The reason the German people are not even aware of this, despite having Drivers Licences, Passports and other documents purportedly issued by a Second Reich Government is because the illegal government in Berlin is worried about publicity and being exposed and another reason is because the controlled media is silent on the matter!

Until there is a peace treaty, Germany will technically remain a colony of the United States. After the Supreme Headquarters Allied Expeditionary Forces, (SHAEF) accepted Germany's declaration of defeat, it was quick to recognize the legitimacy of the Zweite Deutsche Reich (The Second German Reich) which was claimed to have been illegally displaced by Hitler's Third Reich!

Only when a legitimate government is established and <u>voted for by the people,</u> will Germany have a legitimate government and the present illegal German government will have to stand down. Following the collapse of the East German Democratic Republic, a treaty confirmed that only The Second German Reich, now led by Reichskanzler

(Chancellor) Dr Wolfgang Gerhard Guenter Ebel, represented the legitimate German State, but that is as far as matters went and the 'illegal' government of the Federal Republic of Germany is still very much in power and the real reason for this is not hard to find knowing the precarious legal position of the cherished United Nation's Organization, upon which the hopes of the 'One Worlder's rests! Might this explain the urgent need for the World Order Government to be put in place?

Interestingly, the first law Proclamation No.1, making U.S. General Dwight D. Eisenhower, supreme authority in areas under U.S. Control was signed on Feb. 13, 1944 and these SHAEF laws were to remain in effect for a period of 60 years from date of signing and would apply to all of Europe. This poses the question, what has happened since the laws expired in 2004, if anything? [50]

---

[50]   Information courtesy – www.Rense.com *'Germany still in Jurisdictional Limbo.'*

19. 'COMMANDERS OF ISRAEL'

Notice a timeous warning by the prophet Micah...."*hear, please you heads of Jacob and you Commanders of Israel. Is it not your business to know justice?*

2. You haters of good, lovers of badness........

3. You the ones who have eaten the organisms of <u>my people</u>....*smashed to pieces their bones.*

4. At that time you will call to your God for aid, but he will not answer...he will conceal his face from you at that time.....

So, might now not be the time to seriously rethink the entire World Order issue before it is too late? For certainly Satan has deceived the world. Also, our war is not against *flesh and blood but against...wicked spirit forces* Ephesians 6.12

Notice Roman's Chapter 11 which covers the Apostle Paul becoming an apostle to the nations which brings out God's ultimate plan for both Israel and the nations. Notice verse 25... *I do not want you to be ignorant of this sacred secret... that a dulling of senses has happened on the part of Israel until the full number of people of the nations has come in.*

26. In this manner all Israel will be saved....

32. For God has shut them (Israel and the nations) up altogether in disobedience, **that he might show all mercy**.

33. O the depth of God's riches and wisdom and knowledge....how unsearchable his judgments....To him be glory forever.

Also, this should not be a time for church bashing, or castigating those deceived individuals (those who have allowed themselves to become possessed by demons) who are helping to put a world government in place. Certainly an individual should be free to decide for himself who to serve and whether or not to heed the call to 'Come out of her,' Babylon (Satan's worldwide system of false religion) Is that not the American way? There is no need for squabbling about who is right or wrong. Instead should our efforts not be focused more on attaining to the next level, the Promised Millennium of Peace! Do we need to linger a moment longer in this Satanic 'hell hole' that is our present system is becoming and not move on to real life, of real peace, freedom and being the people we were meant to be, this is not a dream, this is for real and deep down this is what every American knows and wants! That is just who you are and if this message can be properly and effectively communicated, likely it would meet with resounding support and prove to be what America and the world have been waiting for. This has to make sense, this is about survival, that is the big message, the alternatives are simply too horrific to imagine and all that is required to turn things around is a little humility and a whole lot of guts. But it would not be the first time in history that the American people have been in a corner!

So, while this book attempts to expose and show how the world has and is still being deceived by the Satanic infiltration of religion, this should not be taken as a personal attack on anyone. While God loves you as an individual, He may hate the particular system of worship you find yourself in, if your religion is not truly in line with His Word.

20. 'YOU PETER' ..... A SATANIC DECEPTION

THAT SATAN HAS USED BIBLICAL INFORMATION TO PROJECT LIES INTO THE WORLD IS UNFORTUNATELY A SAD REALITY. BY PEOPLE (THE LAITY) NOT BEING ALLOWED TO HAVE A BIBLE AND BY SERMONS BEING GIVEN IN LATIN, THEY WOULD BECOME VICTIMS OF A GREAT DECEPTION; In Mark 16. 13 – 19 Jesus asks....*Who do you men say the Son of man is*

14. Some say John the Baptist, Elias, ...one of the prophets.

15. But what do you say I am?

16. Peter answered ...you are the Christ, Son of the living God.

17. Jesus answered, blessed art thou...flesh and blood did not reveal this to you, but my Father which is in heaven, did.

18. I say unto you that thou art Peter and <u>upon this rock I will build my church</u> *and the gates of hell shall not prevail against it.*

A 'Rock' in the Bible usually refers to a mountain, or a large stone and is found 119 times as such and everytime when it refers to a person, it is used to refer either to God or to Christ. **In this instance Christ would be the 'rock'. He was the stone the builders rejected, not Peter!**

However, notice the following:-.......' *Thou art Peter [Petros – a (piece) of rock, stone or pebble] and upon this Rock [Petra a (mass of) rock] I will build my church.* **Today Pope Benedict XVI is constantly reaffirming that Jesus made St Peter the Rock!**

The task of giving an authentic interpretation of the

Word of God whether in it's written form or in the form of Tradition, has been entrusted to the living teaching office of the Church alone.[51]

Mark 16:18. *And so I tell you Peter you are a rock, and on this rock foundation I will build my church. - Good News Bible.*

The three metaphors to which Jesus takes recourse are very clear in themselves;

- Peter will be the rock foundation upon which the building of the church will be based.
- He will have the keys of the Kingdom of Heaven to open and to close to whom he thinks it is just.
- Finally, he will be able to bind and to loose.

For all times, Peter must be the custodian of the communion with Christ..... Peter the Rock, Vatican City June 7, 2006.

This is not actually Biblical – that is what is put over to the people, but this beast speaks out of both sides of the mouth…..

'Not a single Father can find any hint of a Petrine office in the great Biblical texts that refer to Peter.' <u>Peters supremacy and infallibility so central to the Catholic Church today, are simply not mentioned.</u>

Not a single creed, nor confession, nor catechism, nor passage in patriotic writings contains one syllable about the pope, still less about faith and doctrine being decreed by him.[52]

The entire deception hangs on Mark 16:18 and to this Revelation 17:9 says…..*and Satan deceiveth the whole*

---

51 *Catechism of the Catholic church* # 85
52 'Vicars of Christ' De Rosa, p. 206

world…..

This is a shocking revelation……. "I cannot soften it. I was deceived my entire life until someone had the guts to tell me what the Bible actually says." Again, this is a shocking revelation but please understand that God loves every person, but hates the deception, just like when we speak about Christ and the churches from Ephesus to Laodicea when he said he hated the practices of Nicolaus .

Revelation 18: verse 4 says….*'come out of her my people' so that you will not receive part of her plagues…* notice Revelation 17.16 <u>…….the ten horns you saw and the wild beast, these will hate the harlot and will make her devastated and naked and will…completely burn her with fire….</u> This is a call where Jesus loves you as an individual, but hates the system that you might find yourself in!

Many scriptures can be found in the Bible that clearly show that Jesus would be the 'rock' or cornerstone upon which the church would be built.

In Matthew 21.42….*Jesus said to them."Did you ever read in the Scriptures. The stone that the builders rejected is the one that has become the chief cornerstone! "*

Notice also 1 Peter 2.6 where this is confirmed by Peter himself;…..*For it is contained in scripture; "Look! I am laying in Zion a stone , chosen, a foundation cornerstone, precious and no one exercising faith in it will by any means come to disappointment,"* while in Daniel 2.45 we read…*.'a stone (Jesus)not cut by hands '*

44. *'will crush and put an end to all these kingdoms.'*

21. 'A HAPPY ENDING?' ONLY YOU CAN MAKE THAT HAPPEN!

With the final curtain about to go up on the end of Satan's wicked system and with the promised 'Millennium of Peace' ahead, would it not be wisdom on the part of <u>all you fathers (also all you mothers) to know that it is your God given duty to help your families,</u> your children, your grandchildren to know and understand what is going on, what is about to happen, <u>so that they will not to be deceived into receiving the Mark of the Beast</u>...and will know what to do to survive into the New Millennium. This comes across in Deuteronomy 5 – 25. *'Listen, O Israel...*

6. These words I am commanding you today, must prove to be in your heart...

7. And <u>you must inculcate them in your son</u> and speak of them when you sit in your house .....

12 watch out that you do not forget the Lord who brought you out of the land of Egypt out of the land of slaves.

25 it will mean righteous ....

Lord Monckton, by boldly warning of the grave dangers that lie ahead for America has set a fine example for men of goodwill everywhere to courageously follow by taking a stand for truth and righteousness and with the help of Almighty God, assist in setting matters straight in the world's two great democracies!

While fear inspiring times may lie ahead, it is God's Will that you and your families will all enter the Millennium of Peace.

Might it be that there is will be a happy ending to this great saga, like always happens in the movies? Why not? You can make this happen! <u>Make it your business to share the 'Seek Him Early Message' Hosea 5:15 with family, friends and loved ones as this is the answer to all American AND the world's problems.</u> Do your utmost to keep the Commandments of God which were given for our benefit and to have strong faith in the Salvation Jesus has offered and thus be marked for life! And above all, be obedient to the call from Heaven to; 'Come out of Her!' And yes, let the world know that we all stand for unity, unity in truth and peace and that according to His Word there will be a peaceful new world in the coming millennium.

Again, notice Revelation 12.11....*they conquered him because of the blood of the Lamb and because of the word of their witnessing and they did not love their souls even in the face of death.* This tells us that the battle has already been won, so that a lessening of those days is now a real possibility and the reason for us to start paying urgent attention and to prepare ourselves for what may be <u>a sudden and unexpected return of Jesus and His mighty angels who will remove the wicked and restore righteous to the world....our eyes will merely see it</u>! Is that not in itself a good reason for a 'Revival of Faith?'

So, join those spoken of in Isaiah chapter 2.2....*And it must occur in the final part of the days ...*

7. many will come and say "Come, you people and let us go up to the ...House of the God of Jacob and He will instruct us in His Way. He will set matters straight respecting many people. And they will have to beat their swords into plough shears and their spears into pruning hooks and they will learn war no more!" For the former things have passed away...Revelation 21.1

Revelation 21.4 tells that .....*And he will wipe out every tear from their eyes, and death will be no more, nor mourning, nor pain. The former things will have passed away.*

Notice what is recorded at Roman's 11.25,26.....*I do not want you to be ignorant of this sacred secret that there has been a dulling of sensibility on the part of Israel until the full number of the people of the nations have come in.*

26. In this way all Israel will be saved. As it is written, **the Deliverer** *will come out of Zion and will remove ungodliness from Jacob.*

27. And this will be My Covenant with them when I shall take away their sins.

32. For God has consigned all men to disobedience that He may have mercy on them all [alike.]

This tells us that there will be a happy ending for all mankind in the coming New Millennium. Read about this in your own Bible, in fact read the entire Chapter 11 of the Book of Romans for a better understanding.

22. OTHER VIEWS

Well known British Author, David Icke in his book, *Children of the Matrix* has a different take on what is going on in the world, from an entirely non-religious perspective which I shall attempt to para-phrase; (but either way the choice we have remains the same)

What <u>Creation</u> does so magnificently is put the consequences of our choices, in front of our faces, This imperfect world is a consequence of human choice, the choice of those who wish to control and the choices of those that sit back and let them do it, or close their minds to what is happening because they think it is easier that way.

So creation is presenting the consequences of our action or inaction and it is this that makes the world we live in absolutely perfect because we are experiencing what we need to experience. Two apparent opposites, but both are true.

In reality, it is all just a game. A cosmic game called evolution, <u>a game called love.</u>

In this game the longer we stay in denial, the more powerful and challenging the consequences will become. People are hurting, economies are down and until this situation is addressed and turned around, the suffering will continue.

That is our choice. The question is how extreme must the consequences become, before we act?

"We are not humans on a spiritual journey. We are spiritual beings on a human journey. **Stephen Covey.**

So, either way America is at cross-roads and 'We the

People' need to make a choice, to do nothing and stay in denial or to stand up and say 'No' to the global fascist state and it's sponsors who are foisting it upon us, regardless of the consequences. What has happened to the saying that... 'these colors don't run?

Other books by the author that are currently available on www.Amazon.com:

'In God We Trust' Written in 1996 and published in 2000...... *warning the American people that something would trigger America's 'roller coaster ride' down to the Biblical Great Tribulation followed by Armageddon. Sadly, a year later the events of 9/11 proved to be that 'trigger.'*

'A Rush To War' published 2010.......*written for the British people and tells how some good may have come by the War in Iraq becoming protracted and sheds some light on what is described as the World's Greatest Scam.'*

NOW 'God's Final Call' A tribute to Mark Woodman published 2011 (extracts of which you have been reading) *tells of a war of deception that is moving into it's final phase and explains how our leaders, our elite, even our churches have put a padlock on any mention of this, when in fact even they have fallen into a trap and have got it all wrong and are taking us down a slippery slope of no return that will result in billions of lives being lost, if not stopped.* **Even a warning given by the late Pope John Paul II about this seems to have been ignored** .....*this is truly news breaking, must read stuff....*

Sadly, Mark died at the early age of 34 years after struggling with cancer. Any who have watched his DVD's that are available on info@homebase.org will know what an incredible speaker he was!

To become a '*Friend and Lover of Freedom*' there are no formalities, you simply make it your business to be one and to share the truth with family and friends. In need obtain further copies of this book from the person you received your copy from or visit the following website www.Lulu.com/JustDone

Before closing notice a little more about our unseen enemy

Sincerely,
Robert M. Wettergreen

THE FOLLOWING ARE EXTRACTS FROM 'A RUSH TO WAR' THAT WILL SHOW MORE ABOUT WHAT IS GOING ON BEHIND THE SCENE;

To put matters into greater perspective let's turn back the clock and run through the events that seem to have led up to the present situation;

THE PRE HISTORY WORLD

- On ancient Sumerian tablets the name of the leader of the 'reptilian gods' who was said to be from the Sirius and Orion part of the galaxy (from a planet Nibiru) was An of the Anunnakki. UFO researchers

seem to agree with this.
- Zulu legend tell of a 'gigantic war' on Sirius where humans drove these ones out.
- Atlantean (Atlantis) legends tell of a very dark force (these ones) who took over power and used their advanced knowledge to create absolute mayhem and terror. Some have suggested that it was their manipulation of energy that caused the energy imbalances that resulted in the cataclysmic events including the flood or deluge that ended ancient Atlantis and what is known as the 'Golden Age' that had lasted hundreds of thousands of years.
- It is thought that how this happened was that part of Jupiter broke away in a collision with another planet that once orbited between Mars and Jupiter. This body has since become known as Venus. The impact of the collision caused Jupiter to veer through the solar system and throw the outer planets into disarray. The debris from the collision also resulted in the creation of – the asteroid belt.
- After devastating Mars, the Venus comet made several orbits of the earth causing tidal waves and devastation that ended Atlantis and caused the sudden freezing of the poles. It is also suggested that the earth was much closer to the sun prior to this event and that Mars was located on the present orbit of the earth. Mars Space Missions have confirmed that Mars once enjoyed a warmer climate. So it would seem that Venus was squeezed in between the Earth and Mercury, forcing both the Earth and

Mars to move a little further away from the Sun. There are ancient astrological records where Venus is not mentioned, while in later records she is, as if confirming that it was only recently, within the last 5,000 to 10,000 years that she arrived in her present position. There is also evidence to suggest that both the Earth and Mars were once hotter than they are at present. There are accounts of mammals found in a frozen state in Siberia with green grass still in their mouths, indicating that the environmental changes happened instantaneously. Similarly it would appear that Mars was once habitable and had flowing water that is now frozen.

- The devastation of the earth resulted in civilization having to start over again. This happened in the region of Mesopotamia where the ancient civilization of Sumer has since become known as the 'cradle of civilization.'
- **It was from this region that God called Abraham and told him to leave the land and journey to a distant land where He would make him Father of His Chosen or Covenant people Israel.** By so doing, God put into action His plan to counter the challenge the 'wicked one' had made against His Universal Sovereignty and Right to Rule His Creation that will be decided at Armageddon.
- There is also evidence in ancient tablets found in Sumeria showing that the 'wicked one' was soon back in action behind the scene after the flood manipulating world events as it's unseen ruler.

Despite much of this having been documented in perhaps hundreds of books and on websites, even in the Bible[53] the ordinary person seems to know very little about it.

We are about to see how God will finally act to bring an end to this 'rebellion' by one third of his angels (the demons) and their leader Satan. According to the Scriptures this will be God's war Armageddon, our eyes will merely see it. There will be Great Tribulation as never before.

This is not how the world's media likely will portray matters, instead there will probably much hype and hot-air about the virtues of the world order government and what it will do for humanity. The deception will continue right up until Armageddon.

HITLER THE PERFECT EXAMPLE OF AN ILLUMINATI OPERATIVE IN ACTION

Let's pause and see how these ones operate and take a fresh look at recent World history and at Hitler who undoubtedly was one of the world's notorious characters and look at the forces that brought him to power. These are very brief extracts from 'Children of the Matrix' by David Icke.

There is no better example of how Illuminati Bloodlines possessed by demonic entities operate than that of Adolf Hitler. It is believed that Hitler was actually of the Rothschild

---

[53] Notice 2 Peter 3.5...'*this fact escapes them, that there were heavens from of old and an earth of old standing compactly out of water and in the midst of water by the word of God.*' This would seem to imply that in former days there was one solid land mass surrounded by water as opposed to separate continents as there are today.

bloodline. The Illuminati produce many offspring out of wedlock and place them into positions of power.

Austrian Chancellor Dolfuss found from official registration cards of house servants that an innocent young servant girl with the surname that happened to be Hitler had fallen pregnant while working for Salomon Mayer Rothschild, in Vienna. He had a lecherous passion for young girls and there were instances when his adventures had to be hushed up by the police. The story continues but the short of it is that this child was Adolf Hitler!.

When standing on a public platform with that contorted face and crazed delivery, he was channeling the "reptilian demonic" consciousness and transmitting this vibration to vast crowds. 'One cannot help thinking of him as a medium.' For most of the time, mediums are ordinary, insignificant people. Suddenly, they are endowed with what seems to be supernatural powers, which set them apart from the rest of humanity. Hitler was possessed by forces outside of himself. He appeared to live in perpetual fear of "supermen."

Hitler once said to an aide; "What will the social order of the future be like? Comrade I will tell you. There will be a class of overlords……he goes on recounting the hierarchy, the conquered until at the top he mentions an exalted nobility of whom I cannot speak; The new man is living among us now! He is here. I have seen the new man. He is intrepid and cruel.I was afraid of him."

Hitler was a member of both the Thule and Vril Secret Societies and spent a lot of time in Barvaria whence the Illuminati had sprung. A big influence on Hitler was the Bulwer-Lytton's novel *The Coming Race*. This is about an enormous civilization inside the earth well ahead of our own. These underground supermen would according to Bulwer-Lytton's novel emerge on the surface one day and take control of the world. The theme of underground supermen or "Hidden Masters" can be found in most secret societies legends around the world

Dietrict Eckart, a heavy drinker and drug taking writer met Hitler in 1919 and decided he was the 'one', the Messiah he was looking for. It was Eckart who is credited with Hitler's advanced esoteric knowledge and black magic rituals that plugged him so completely into the demonic reptilians. From now on, Hitler's power to attract support grew rapidly Eckart wrote to a friend in 1923.

Also of note is that the Nazis did not disappear in 1945, they just went underground. The inner core of the Nazi secret society network was the Black Order which continues today and is reported to be the innermost circle of the CIA. Allen Dulles the first head of the CIA was a Nazi supporter and he was a key force behind Operation Paperclip that protected Nazis like Josepf Mengele after the war and took them to America. The Dulles family were cousins of the Rockefellers (bloodline in other words), Reinhard Gehlen the man appointed by Dulles to set up the CIA network in Europe, was one of Hitler's SS chiefs. Only Nazis considered expendable were sent to the Nuremberg show trials designed to cover up what happened.

The original swastika, an ancient Sun symbol was right-handed, which in esoteric terms, means light and creation, the positive. The Nazis reversed this to symbolize the left-hand path – black magic and destruction.

So, here the King of the North mentioned in the Prophecy of Daniel Chapter II it would seem is alive and well. Does this mean that God's people are without hope and will soon be at the mercy of the dark forces that are behind the coming UN World Government?

At this late hour these ones would be wise to do whatever necessary to hold on to their countries God given Sovereignty's and above all to "Seek Him Early" Hosea 5.15. and to trust that the Hand of Providence that has never failed, will again be there for His people in their time of need!

If you are one who would be upset by graphic details and descriptions about what is going on behind the scene you may be a little apprehensive about viewing the information that follows that may be a little too insensitive to your liking. However, by the same token you could regard it as educational. So prepare yourself to take a brief look behind the scene into the 4th dimension from where the unseen ruler of the world and his cohorts operate.

THE 4TH DIMENSION

To help understand a little about the dynamics of such inter-dimensional covert control we need to understand that we are in the third dimension and they operate from the fourth, a frequency just outside the range of our physical senses. (sight, sound, touch, taste and smell.) You might think of it as a kind of parallel universe.

Like radio waves that we cannot see and are all around

us, that can pass through windows and walls, so too can these entities that share our space and can move in and out of our dimension at will.

Einstein tells us that matter is merely energy condensed to a slow state of vibration. Our minds observe the visible and physical world and only what we perceive becomes our reality, and not in fact what really is!

In the Bible there are several references to indicate that Satan and his demons would be in our midst, notably;

John 14.30 where Jesus says..."*the ruler of the world is coming. And he has no hold on me."*

Revelation 12.7. *And war broke out in heaven; Michael and his angels battled with the dragon, and the dragon and its angels battled but it did not prevail........*

9. *So down the great dragon was hurled, the original serpent, the one called Devil and Satan, who is misleading the entire inhabited earth, and his angels were hurled down with him.**

12 *On this account be glad you heavens...Woe to the earth and for the sea, because the Devil has come down to you, having great anger, knowing he has a short period of time.*

2 Peter 2.4. ..... *God did not hold back from punishing the angels that sinned.... by throwing them into Tartarus, delivered them to pits of dense darkness to be reserved for judgment....*

Job 1.6...*God said to Satan: "Where do you come from?" At that Satan answered..."from roving about in the earth and walking about on it."* So, he is right here in our midst.

Also notice Ephesians 6.12..*we have a wrestling not*

against blood and flesh, but against governments and authorities, against the rulers of this darkness, against wicked spirit forces ……

We are not alone! While we may think that we live in our own world or universe, it is confirmed in Scripture that the world is actually being controlled and has been controlled for millenniums by the unseen 'wicked creature' Satan and his demons and also his earthly agents. Those 'possessed' who do his bidding.

In former times and right down through history they operated openly through kings and emperors through the 'Divine Right of Kings.' Today, they do not openly manifest themselves, rather it is done covertly through a net- work of secret societies that collectively make up a pyramid type structure with the Illuminati at its top, which is run by some of the most famous and well known people on the planet.

Being relatively few in number the Anunnaki (An, Lucifer or Satan and his demons) the extraterrestrials invaders of the planet need the Church and the Illuminati as a front for them to carry out their agenda for the creation of a planetary dictatorship with us humans as a type of micro-chipped robotic mind controlled slave population.

This would account for reports of their bizarre genetic experiments in hidden facilities, one described or known as 'nightmare hall' on Level Six at the Dulce underground base in New Mexico. (The following information was published in LIFO magazine by Researchers Bill Hamilton and TAL Levesque , also known as Jason Bishop III.)

Inside Dulce there are Genetic Labs, Reports from workers tell of seeing bizarre multi-legged "humans" or half human, half octopus. Also reptilian humans and a vast range of humanoid creatures half-human, half lizard, winged humanoids, grotesque bat like creatures, furry reptilian creatures with human hands that cry like babies.{one worker said}...I frequently encountered humans in cages usually half dazed or drugged, but sometimes they cried and begged for help. We were told they were hopelessly insane and involved in high-risk drug tests to cure insanity. We were told never to try to speak to them.

According to Phil Schneider the son of a German U-boat commander in the Second World War, he knew of 131 underground military bases, an average of one mile deep in the United States constructed for the New World Order Agenda financed by what is called as the 'Black Budget!'

Schneider also told that under the new Denver International airport, east of Denver, there are several main levels underneath, at least ten sub-levels, a 4.5 square mile underground city, and an 88.5-square mile underground base. The Denver base is said to include massive "containment camps" for holding "dissents." Workers who experienced the deeper levels of the base saw scenes so terrifying they refused to talk about them. From other sources these bases are where many millions of children who go missing every year world- wide are taken. They are used for slave labour and eaten by the reptilians, just like humans eat chicken or cows.

Might this indicate and confirm the desperation on the part of the reptilians to transform themselves into humans perhaps to escape God's wrath? Or vice-versa. There has to be a reason for it. Also for their need to consume vast amounts of blood to sustain their hormone levels and to keep their DNA codes open in order to maintain human form?

To help understand these ones we know that until the eight week the human fetus goes through many stages of development similar to non-human species before taking its evolutionary path as a human. At one stage the embryo develops gills, even a caudal appendage or tail.

So too in the development of the human brain is the development of a reptilian component, the 'R-complex. It is from this ancient reptilian part of the human brain that we get our cold-blooded character traits. Characteristics such as 'territoriality' (this is mine, get out) aggression; and the idea that 'might is right, winner – takes all.' These are the very attitudes of the Illuminati.

Scientists say that the R-Complex represents a core of the nervous system and originates from a 'mammal-like reptile' that was once found all over the world in the Triassic period (250-240 million years ago.) All mammals have this reptilian part of the brain.

Fortunately, unlike in reptiles this part of the human brain is balanced by other parts, so we are not completely cold-blooded or unfeeling. There is so much more about the reptilian species that could be discussed that would fill volumes.

Albert Einstein gave us his theory $E=MC^2$ showing that matter is a form of energy and that energy cannot be destroyed, only transformed into another state. Matter is just energy condensed to a slow state of vibration. X-Ray technology is simply a tuning device that tunes into frequencies that match our bone structure or in the case of say a building can show the reinforcing steel frame by tuning into that frequency.

It is a basic scientific fact that energy cannot be destroyed, but can change form by changing the temperature (frequency) as in the case of ice where ice becomes water and water steam.

Modern technology can show that our human aura, even our thoughts and emotions (frequencies) are a mass of different colours (frequencies) that change as our thoughts and emotions change.

So, our very consciousness, is energy and is indestructible, but sadly modern day science and medicine has advanced not beyond this point. While scientists know that 90% of the mass of existence within the atom that is referred to as 'dark matter' is not subject to the laws of gravity and those of the electromagnetic field they have not progressed further by taking the laws of physics that apply to our known frequencies and on this basis judge what is possible in other frequencies.

The term 'dark matter' refers to only what does not reflect light in our frequency range and cannot be seen. The question that really needs to be considered is 'does everything have to reflect light?'

So we continue to live in our own dimension limited to what our five senses perceive as reality. Our minds observe only the visible, physical world and in the process allow the enemy to use this to their advantage and they will continue doing so until our appreciation of reality and 'what really is' changes.

We are more than our physical bodies. Plato said that

all bodies are only the shadows of true reality. Modern or 'Conventional' medicine is purely reactionary and concentrates on the symptons and ignores the causes or multi-frequency forces like thought and emotion that can cause the disharmony or physical diseases.

The point is that we are certainly more than our bodies. We are part of an infinite energy, we are all energy.

There is so much more to this, even the divisions between us are illusions. If we loved each other, there would be no conflict in the world. Neither would the Illuminati be able to manipulate us to look outside ourselves for answers that they know we will never find.

That is why we follow them like sheep believing that the solutions they offer like new laws and new powers even the World coming together as One under a UN World Government will work when in fact it will only succeed in destroying us!

Thus the need to look to a higher source of power for the answers we need and for the power to change both our inner and outer-selves and attitudes with love, God is love! We were created in His image, to mirror and reflect His love in our lives, only then will our reality become the reality that we are struggling to find!

Credo Mutwa believes that the reptilians originated on this planet and were driven off before returning to claim what they believe is rightfully theirs.

To any who find the idea of a reptilian race to be unimaginable Carl Sagan is quoted as saying, "There are more potential combinations of DNA [physical forms] than there are atoms in the universe." "Far from it being impossible for such a race to emerge, it would be more surprising if it had not."

In medicine it has been said that in the United States doctors are now statistically more dangerous than guns. We have a situation where people are actually in hospitals because of the effects of drugs that are supposed to make them well! In the London Daily Mail it was reported that where the cause of death is a hospital acquired infection that this is kept hidden from patients' families and not mentioned on the death certificate! Also, the so called "super-bugs" have mutated immunity to many antibiotics because doctors have been prescribing them like confetti for so long – another behind the scene Illuminati plan to destroy the effectiveness of the human immune system in obedience to their unseen masters. Surely, it is time for change!

It has also been said that Science is now a fascist club in which all members must stay in line. So too is it with the medical profession. The whole 'scientific system' is structured to suppress knowledge because the Illuminati is desperate for us to remain in ignorance of who we are and the true nature of life and who we really are!. If enough people knew the truth, (what you are now reading), their game would be up!

So, how about you professionals who may now be retired, who may have known what has been going on during your careers, but have had to bite your bottom lip rather than expose this evil to preserve your lively-hoods and for the sake of your loved ones. Is it not time to start sharing your experiences and telling it like it really is. Why not even band together with former colleagues and have your stories told.

Can you honestly say that this is really the world you want to leave for your children, if not why not try to make a difference by doing whatever you can to help turn the situation around?

Know that the Millennium of Peace and Righteousness will soon be at hand and also that Justice demands that there are limits even to God's patience, know that He will act!

But, know also that it is God's will that men of all sorts should be saved and come to an accurate knowledge of the truth. .

Also, would you want your loved ones to follow you and the rest of deceived humanity into destruction at Armageddon, surely not? Why, because you love them and want only the very best for them, which is exactly what God wants for you. Why, because you are part of His human family and because God is love, He loves us, despite all! But Justice demands that he act and He will at Armageddon!

Is history repeating itself? In the run up to the Second World War in Britain much of what we are now experiencing was going on back then. There were the few desperately trying to warn about Hitler's Nazi Germany and where matters were heading, while for the majority it was a case of anything for peace, the cry was "Peace in Our Time." Fortunately, as had previously happened before in British history during the time of the Spanish Armada, it was the resolute stand taken by Queen Elizabeth I, that preserved the Sovereignty of England and was instrumental in preventing England from becoming part of the Spanish Catholic Empire, thus allowing Britain to go on to become a first rate naval power with an empire upon which the sun would never set and also to establish the thirteen colonies that would become the New England States and the cornerstone upon which the United States was built!

Likewise, it was Churchill who later took a similar position before and during the Second World War only to be booted out of office once the war was over by the very same crowd of deceived individuals who had tried to block him from taking the nation to war. Are things any different this time around? Is it not the same evil forces that are determined as ever to foist the One World government upon us and if they are not challenged, they will surely succeed. At this late stage having infiltrated what remains of the once 'free-world' there really is not much standing in their way. Needless to say that should not provide a reason for you to surrender your God given sovereignty!

It is through placemen occupying positions of power in big government, business and religion that the Illuminati agenda is carried out. Yes, Satan's tactics never change, why because they work! It's always about money and power and man's lust for it. (the R-Complex at work within us!) So it is that these ones that control every aspect of our lives, set the norms and demand blind conformity and obedience by the human 'herd.' Do not allow yourself to be suckered into following the 'lemming run' over the cliff into oblivion at Armageddon because that is what is where matters are heading!

The evil is incredible, the mental, emotional and physical onslaught, the manipulation of virtually every aspect of our lives. It's all about control. The finger prints of our unseen controllers are in evidence everywhere. In medicine, the drug cartels with their intellect suppressing and mind destroying drugs, aspartame, prozac, ritalin, dumping fluoride into water, immune destroying vaccines, the aids scam, pandemic brain tumors, pseudo heart attacks. Education 2000- iron fisted control of the curriculum, control of science, control of the environment, is further evidence of their manipulation. Global 2000, the New American Century...programs designed to destroy the ability for 'critical thinking,' while promoting and encouraging the 'herd' mentality, knowing that people generally, like 'sheep' are followers.... Also programs for biological warfare against the population and the food supply....to stop people from being mentally, emotionally and physically healthy, the list goes on and on.

The Illuminati's control of money translates into them controlling the world. <u>The problems of poverty, debt, war are made to happen because it makes humanity easier to control.</u>

'Allow me to issue and control the money of a nation, and I care not who writes the law' .....Mayer Amschel Rothschild.

It has been said that after 9/11 beneath one of the Twin Towers, were tunnels which served as a major terminal between the underground society and the surface society it controls.

Also, underneath most major cities especially in the US are subterranean counterpart cities. Similar facilities exist in many other countries around the world in Central and South America, Britain, Egypt, Mesopotamia, Turkey, Asia, China, Malta and elsewhere. High speed monorail trains connect the systems.

Timothy Good in his book *Unearthly Disclosures* confirms

the existence of other extraterrestrial bases. The reliability of these sources was supported by Admiral of the Fleet, Lord Hill-Norton, the former chief of the UK Defence Staff and former chairman of the NATO Military Committee.

Many bases that are underwater exist in Australia, the Pacific, the former Soviet Union, the USA and the Caribbean. These are permanent alien bases. He also said they were 'messing' with plate tectonics, the movement of land that causes earthquakes, as in Tsunami's. Also that the warming of the world's oceans was connected to extraterrestrial activity - it was not global warming that was causing the problem.

In many instances, members of the military above the rank of major are aware of the situation but are sworn to secrecy. Is this the kind of world order you would want to live in?

The white unmarked aircraft seen on many airport runways around the world are there not without a reason! As are the 'Concentration or Detainment Centres' and Re-Education Centres, that are rumored to be spread out across America under Rex-84 and also in other countries and parts of the world? Operation 'Night Train' code name for a nation-wide pre-dawn round up of those considered undesirable or unsuitable for the New World Order.

The Fincen Mission, a U.N./U.S. Program for 'House to house search and seizure of property and arms, A 'separation and categorization' of people as prisoners in large numbers, especially those considered as dangerous to 'Law and Order' because they are not ready to collaborate with the implementation of a New World Order. The huge data bases that are said to exist containing every-ones information. Super computers in Brussels and America! All this and only muted silence from...We the People!

So that is the big picture showing what really is going on. This ungodly world is wicked, sick and it's ruler evil, so be resolved in your heart to '*Seek Him Early*' Hosea.. 5.15.

THE MAYAN CALENDAR

The base resonant frequency of the planet, discovered in 1899 and known as the Schumann Cavity Resonance, remained pretty constant until the mid - 1980s <u>when it began to quicken rapidly</u>...the effect of these higher vibrations is that 'time' appears to be passing much faster. The Maya peoples of Mexico in Yucatan left records of the measurement of time...small, medium and great circles of the Earth's evolution. **One of the great cycles is due to be completed in 2012**. The vibrational frequency of the planet is changing as it completes this vast cycle and enters another. Some call the new cycle...the Age of Aquarius as the earth moves through the area of the heavens dubbed 'Pices.' Some researchers, physics and mystics suggest that our frequency is getting closer every day to the fourth - dimensional range. **This will explain why the reptilians are having to work harder to hold human form and thus the urgency for completion of their agenda** which is the complete control of the planet and to turn its peoples into mind controlled slaves. The human micro-chip called Digital Angel (Angel-Reptilian) Apple-Digital, is already ahead of schedule. Dr Peter Zhou chief scientist of DigitalAngel.net of course has stressed the benefits of people becoming human robots controlled and connected by satellite, according to him implants will become as popular as cell phones. One of his most chilling statements was that DA will be a connection from yourself to the electronic world...your guardian and protector.

This ties in with what the Mayan Mexican Indians refer to as the 'final baktun' that explains that, driven by ego, materialism and money, history and mankind will have reached a kind of saturation point, where history simply will have nowhere to go!! So certainly, for us it is a matter of faith to know that God's Millennium of Peace is at hand!

Zulu historian, Credo Mutwa in his book *Song of the Stars* provides a similar account of space aliens that the Zulu's call the Mzungu, the 'Watchers,' reptilian men with lizard like faces, living in the 'kingdom of the shadows, in the 4th dimension outside the human frequency wave bands who are able to enter or exit our dimension or reality at will.

That certain leading politicans, banking and business leaders, media owners, heads of the military and others are serpents in human form (are possessed by demon entities.) Staggering as this may seem in the minds of people, to most it would be 'utter nonsense.' As Credo Mutwa explains, 'the union between people from the stars and humanity is depicted in virtually every ancient culture and because the situation for humanity is now so perilous <u>it is more important for people to know about this than for him to keep his vows of silence</u>.

SO TAKE A BRIEF LOOK AT YOUR ROOTS AND WHO YOU REALLY ARE.

Even knowledge of the history of the world's two great democracies and its people spread out around the world has been suppressed, but hopefully the following will provide you with a little insight.

Interestingly the *'Declaration of Arbroath'* the **Scottish Declaration of Independence,**' was drawn up in 1320 A.D. by King Robert the Bruce. This document embodied a Scottish appeal to Pope John XXII to appeal on their behalf to King Edward II of England to allow the Scots to live in peace.

The Declaration states 'the Scots journeyed from Greater Scythia (Russia) by way of the Pillars of Hercules (Gibraltar,) and dwelt for a long while in Spain (Iberia) ….Thence came, twelve hundred years after the people of Israel crossed the Red Sea, to their home in the west where today they live. The Declaration reminds the Pope how the Scots received Christianity: 'Nor would He (Christ) have them confirmed in that faith by merely anyone but by the most gentile saint Andrew, the Blessed Peter's brother. Indicating that the Apostle Andrew followed Jesus' command to go the *'Lost sheep of the House of Israel.'* So it would seem that back then the Scots were aware of their <u>true identity as Israelites</u>.

Is it not strange that Manasseh, the 13th tribe of Israel became the Great Nation America and of equal interest is that the Great Seal of the United States has numerous sets of 13 on it….The eagle holds in its claw an olive branch a symbol of peace with 13 leaves, 13 berries…In it's left talon the eagle holds 13 arrows, upon it's breast shield are 13 bars and 13 stripes and a scroll bearing 13 letters….*E- Plurbis Unim.* **Was it co-incidence that America started with 13 colonies.** Also notice the 13 stars in the 'glory' arranged in the Star of David formation within the cloud representing the *'in dwelling'* of God or in Hebrew the *'shekinah.'* Was the unseen hand of God somehow involved in all this?

Interestingly, on the symbols of the British Coat of Arms written in French between the Lion and the Unicorn are *'Honi soit qui mal y pense'* meaning 'Evil to him who thinks evil' of Britain. Also the inscription, *Dieu et Mon Droit*, ...'*God and my birthright,* 'first used by Richard I of England who was also known also as Richard *Coeur de Leo* - Richard the Lion Heart. Likely, as were the Scots, he too was also aware of his roots, his identity as one of the 'lost sheep of the house of Israel.'

So, understanding who Israel is today is a major key to Bible understanding and the prophecies written for our day that will help us understand our roots and identity and what lies ahead. **Also, it will help us to see that we are and will remain Satan's prime and number one target**. It has always been that way and nothing will change matters.

More importantly, at this eleventh hour, it will help people to see through the 'wicked ones' deceit and his deceptions.

In Isaiah 49.1 referring to Israel God says..."Listen to me O you Islands...far away...

3 ...You are my servant O Israel...the one I have chosen"

Further in Jeremiah 31.10 referring to Israel God says the message must be declared to the islands 'far away' and in verse 7 must be shouted to the 'Chief of the Nations.' So according to scripture Israel would be Chief of the Nations and would be on islands set in the sea far away to the north and west of Jerusalem. A line drawn to the north and west of

Jerusalem takes us directly to the British Isles.

In Ezekiel 17.8 we read that the 'seed of the land' would be planted in a *fruitful field by great waters*. Being in the vicinity or next to *great waters* is something that has always been associated with the location of the British Isles.

To understand this we need to recall that it was God's promise to David that down through the generation's and to time indefinite that there would always be a descendant of his wearing the crown.

Notice the second part of Jeremiah's commission *to build and to plant*....this comes across in Ezekiel 17.22 where God says...'I *myself will also take some of the lofty cedar, from the top, I shall pluck off a Tender One and on the MOUNTAIN OF ISRAEL I SHALL TRANSPLANT IT and it will bear boughs and bear fruit and become a MAJESTIC CEDAR. And under it will reside all birds of every wing.*

Through the prophet Jeremiah, God was going to take a tender young twig - a daughter of King Zedekiah of the Southern Kingdom of Judah and plant it on a mountain (nation) ...the Northern ten tribed Kingdom of Israel. This is confirmed in Isaiah 37.31...*those who escape of the house of Judah...will certainly take root downward and produce fruit upward.* Lost Israel would again become a self-ruling nation and in time would spread around the world gaining dominion and power.

Irish history also tells the story of an elderly white haired patriarch sometimes referred to as a saint or prophet sometimes referred to as *Ollam Falla* who arrived in Ireland around 580 BC accompanied by a princess daughter of an eastern king and a companion Simon Barach. The Princess had a Hebrew name Tea-Tephi (*daughter of God's House* - or in Irish *Lughaidh* - *Lug* Celtic for God and *Aidh* for house.)

The royal party included the son of the King of Ireland (an Israelite of the tribe of Dan?) who had been in Jerusalem at the time it fell to the Babylonians. The royal husband of Princess Tephi was given the title Hereman. King Herreman and the Hebrew Princess continued on the throne of Ireland and the same dynasty continued unbroken through all the kings of Ireland, before being overturned and transplanted to Scotland and overturned a third time and moved to London, England where the same dynasty continues today.

According to Irish historian Thomas Moore[54] the earliest residents of Ireland, the Firbolgs were dispersed by '*Tuantha de Danaan*' or tribe of Dan who had migrated from Greece (Danoi of Greece) around 1200B.C. Another Irish historian Geoffrey Keating cites a further wave of Danaan immigrants to Ireland around the 8th Century B.C. at about the time of the Assyrian invasion of the Northern Kingdom of Israel. History of Ireland[55].

So it would seem that Ireland was home from home for Israel, having first settled there as far back as the 8th century B.C., and it would be a reasonable to conclude that the son of the King of Ireland who was to marry the Hebrew princess was himself of the tribe of Dan and of the Northern Kingdom of Israel and would therefore be of the Zarah line.

Jeremiah brought with him other items of interest, a harp, an arch and a stone called 'Lail;Fail' or stone of destiny. Later the kings of Ireland, Scotland and England were coronated sitting over this stone including the present Queen. Until

54   *History of Ireland*, Vol 1, p.59
55   Vol 1 p.159 - 199

recently the stone rested in Westminster Abbey, London with the coronation chair built over it. It bore the label - 'Jacob's Pillar Stone' referred to in Genesis 28.18. The stone was however returned to Scone, Scotland in 1996.

Interestingly, King Edward I referring to the Coronation Stone, said "It is the one primeval monument which binds together the whole empire."

Sir Walter Scott referring to this *'Precious Relic'* in line with the inscription on the stone penned the following prophetic verse....

> *"Unless the fates are faithless grown*
> *And prophet's voice be vain*
> *Where'er is found this sacred stone*
> *The Wanderer's Race shall reign."*

Through three hundred generations men have felt that Jacob's Pillar Stone was a thing worth dying for in battle.

Of the struggle of the Anglo-Saxons westward it has been written there could be *no grander theme upon the scrolls of history. The very streams of Europe mark their resting places, and the root of their ancient names.*

When reflecting on this, it all seems so truly amazing and inspiring that the words of that well known English Hymn, Jerusalem come to mind;

> *'And did those feet in ancient times*
> *Walk on England's mountain's green*
> *And was the Holy Lamb of God*
> *On England's pleasant pastures seen.'*

Certainly the answer to the question *'And did those feet walk on England's mountain's green?* would be a resounding 'Yes,' all things being considered as brought out so far in our discussion. Notice what Jesus had to say about the 'lost sheep.'

At Matthew 15.24 Jesus said…. '<u>I was not sent to any but to the lost sheep of the house of Israel</u>." So by this being his very first instruction to his disciples, clearly shows that it was an important priority. "

Notice also Matthew 10 verse 5 these twelve Jesus sent forth giving them orders…Do not go off into the road of the nations….

6. But go <u>continually to the lost sheep of the house of Israel</u>…

God wanted His Chosen People Israel to become a living example to all nations showing that His ways, with Love ,Justice, Kindness and Mercy at their very centre were far superior to Satan's **'Survival of the fittest,' 'Winner takes all'** ways!

It is for this reason that I would like humbly and in all sincerity, to have a quiet and friendly 'conversation' with you. If this is not a good time, just put a bookmark in at this place, so that when you do have time for some quiet reflection you may come back to it.

As most folk today really have little knowledge of Bible prophecy the purpose of our little chat would simply be to go through the facts with you as an open-minded thinking person, privately, without solicitation or commitment, to help you make the most important decision that you will ever make be required to make in all eternity.

It's about the issues; siding either with God or with Satan and about free will; every living soul will soon have to make the decision whether or not to accept what the scriptures refer to as the 'mark of the beast.' It has been said that this could take the form of some type of micro-chip implant device. But what it really will involve is in some way consciously bowing down to Satan and accepting his system. Unfortunately, most of unsuspecting humanity will not see any problem in accepting the mark. But as mentioned earlier **their names have not been written in the '*book of life*'** and they will thus forgo their hope of eternity and will be among those who Satan will take down with him at Armageddon!

This is something every living soul needs to know about, but few do while most are completely in the dark about it!

For some 6,000 years God has patiently endured the rebellion of his former spirit sons and also of humanity and has had to observe the most diabolical acts of violence and immorality, perversions of every description, despicable blasphemies against His very person. So, standing at the threshold of the coming 'Seventh Day Millennium of Peace and Righteous' would it not be wisdom on the part of people to start taking note rather than to allow themselves to be deceived into foregoing the opportunity to enter this 'day of rest?'

What people need to know is that, Satan throughout time has been intent on destroying God's people. Nothing has changed apart from us having allowed ourselves to play right into his hands by getting ourselves so completely caught up in his fast paced secular world that we are totally unaware about what is really going on!

Notice Psalm 83.4....."***Come let us efface them from being a nation that the name of Israel may be remembered no more***..."

That is what Satan's true intention is, but like stubborn children and by ignoring our Maker's Handbook, the Bible, we cannot see where our independent spirit has led us and how we have played right into the 'wicked ones' hands and fallen into the trap that he has set to ensnare and destroy us.

God's blessings have come and gone with little or no proper appreciation and we are now in the time of the Malediction's.

What does the record show as regards us observing God's Commandments. Well, can it be denied that the aspersions cast as regards the First and Greatest Commandment – that God's Great Name Yaweh, Jah, Jehovah should actually be covered up is simply incredible, but there it is!. Certainly, the wars and bloodshed over the centuries bear testimony to our neglect as regards the second commandment. Also, that the 'land of the free' the great Protestant Nation that was built by those fleeing the persecutions of the Roman Church's Inquisition, would Not promulgate laws that would actually uphold the sanctity of the Fourth Commandment and the keeping of the Sabbath and would actually follow the errant ways of the church in worshipping God on the pagan Sunday, to say the least is in itself quiet ironic, if it were not for the dark forces that hold sway over our actions. As regard the other commandments, the 'Thou Shalt Not 'Kill, Steal, Commit Adultery, Covet, Bear False Witness, Worship Idols……and even our stewardship of the planet what does the record show? Also, what does the record show as regards God's dealing with such rebellion on our part…… nothing but love, repeated undeserved kindness, mercy and great forbearance!

Thus the 'Seek Him Early ' message Hosea 5.15 as it will only be through our sincere prayers and entreaties that God will finally act to put an end to Satan's reign of terror at Armageddon. Or will we simply do nothing and allow Satan to have his way and us accepting the Reptilian fascist state?

Because of the 'free will' issue, the matter is entirely in our hands. But through our continued stubbornness likely we will have to undergo much unnecessary and avoidable pain and suffering before we finally 'Get It.' But, we have the assurance that *'in our dire straits'* we will *'Seek His Face.'*

So **please**, know that it is going to happen and know what to do to survive, no matter how hard it may be as this is your only hope. Also, you need have no doubt the Holy Bible, despite all the human and demonic propaganda that has been used to distort and destroy it's truth. It will not fail. If considered properly and seriously, there is no other book that comes close to accurately foretelling future events.

LESSONS LEARNT - THE WAR IN IRAQ

If **any good** has come out of the **War in Iraq** by it becoming protracted, it most certainly would be that it has delayed the implementation of the World Order Government that was supposed to have been in place soon after the turn of the century early in 2011. The Iraq was only planned to have lasted six months and this has provided a window of opportunity for the real truth about what is going to happen to come out

God has warned us that He is going to act and when He

does, there will be no stopping Him, ***it will be final***!

Yet general apathy is everywhere in evidence. In Matthew 24 verse 37 - 39 concerning our times Jesus compared these to *the days of Noah*

38. *As they were before the flood eating and drinking, marrying* (normal everyday stuff) *until the day that Noah entered the ark*

39 *and they took no note until the flood came and swept them away .so the presence of the Son of man will be.*

There is A BIG LESSON in this for all of us and really is the point of writing this. Saddam Hussein's self-centered rebellion and defiance in the face of authority mirrors that of another, the unseen wicked spirit creature and fallen angel, Satan, who Jesus in John 14.30 referred to as 'the ruler of the world,' who for his own selfish reasons has made life so difficult for mankind down through the ages. Like Saddam, he too knows that his time will soon be up, but he would rather take humanity down with him into destruction, than to admit and accept defeat and while not realized by most, that is precisely what he is up to at present. **Would this once more be a case of us not 'knowing the enemy?'**

What he is planning, definitely has nothing to do with him eagerly wanting to patronize and assist in bringing to fruition the obsession of those dearly departed empire building old-timers for a 'World Order' that would bring the world and it's people into a state of perfect peace and harmony.

Again, that is not what he does. He is a destroyer, he does not build or create, to the contrary, he destroys. If that were his mission, he likely would have been achieved that long ago? By his (Satanic) propaganda and lies, he has succeeded in totally deceiving all mankind even our trusted leaders.

Everything about him is diametrically opposed to truth and goodness. Yet, seldom if ever is he even mentioned, and when he is, it is usually as a 'harmless' cartoon character dressed in red with horns and a pitch-fork in hand, rather than man-kinds most deadliest enemy. Again, are we not on a collision course with a calamity of unknown proportions, simply because we 'Do not know our number one enemy?'

Mostly, it is as if he simply does not exist that he has succeeded in shifting the blame for anything that happens on to God, whose goodness, virtue and moral excellence is 'Goodness to the absolute sense.' Psalm 25.8. In Romans 1.20 The Apostle Paul attempts to explain God's total awesomeness and really incomprehensible power. ....*His invisible qualities are clearly seen in creation by the things (He) created from the smallest of cells to billions upon billions of huge galaxies.* Further in Ecclesiastes 3.11 we read... *everything he has made...even time indefinite he has put in their hearts, that mankind may never find out the work that the true God has made...*

Created in God's likeness and image are His earthly children and He wants us to learn about Him and His creation. He wants us, as it were to advance to the next level in this our cosmic journey into eternity. Are we not truly blessed? Will the soon to come millennium of peace be the first phase in that journey?

In Isaiah 45.18 we read *the true God the Former of the earth. He who firmly established it who did not create it simply for nothing.*

19. *I spoke not to the seed of Jacob, 'Seek me simply*

for nothing.' Further in Isaiah 55.11 we have the following assurance...***my word goes forth...will prove to be. It will not return to me without results, but it will certainly do that in which I have delighted***.

In 1Timothy 1.11 He is described as...*the happy God* and in Psalm 130.3 we see one of His greatest qualities, that of forgiveness *if errors were what you watched who could stand*. Also Psalm 65.2. *O Hearer of prayer, to you people of all flesh will come*.

So from these few Scriptures we can see that life as we know it today is far removed from the infinite life that God purposed for us in the beginning and that He promises when righteousness is restored to the earth.

The natural desire of people is to live orderly and peaceful lives, yet despite the efforts of countless well meaning individuals, the world has suffered terribly throughout history. This would seem almost a paradox were it not for the presence of an invisible wicked spirit creature manipulating events behind the scene.

Today, demonic forces under Satan's control are behind the scene, everywhere actively, exercising influence, possession and control over human rulers and mankind in general, prompting them to commit unspeakable acts of crime, violence, genocide, terrorism and murder. In fact mankind has become so accustomed to it, that rarely if ever do such things make headlines and are accepted as normal, just as long as it doesn't effect us directly. But we should never develop the mindset that the 'relative peace' we now enjoy will can last in a dangerous and evil world.

Even as this is being written he is behind the scene

manipulating world events to achieve the establishment of the World Order Government that he hopes will ensure his complete and total control of all humanity. Back in Eden he claimed he could turn all of Adam and Eve's yet unborn offspring from God **and that it wasn't possible for God to rule the universe by love as selfishness will always triumph**.

This will be his final attempt to alienate all mankind from God. <u>The intention is that all humanity by having to voluntarily or involuntarily submit themselves to him and thus being marked, will make them his people and will leave God with an 'empty' victory and as it were and will 'put it in God's face.</u>' He will not relent and will remain a rebel to the very end.

From the time of the rebellion in Eden he has wanted all the glory for himself and if he cannot have it, he will make sure that no one does. If this was not the reason then, there simply would be no need for the secrecy that surrounds the New World Order Government.

Perhaps, he still thinks he can win by succeeding in putting in place the New World Order Government under the U.N., which will be the ultimate dictatorship, where every individual will either worship him and conform as some kind of mind controlled robotic slave, or will be removed and killed or in a worst case scenario, if he has to go down he will take the rest of humanity down with him. So the stakes are extremely high!

Imagine a scenario where the authorities of the World Order Government will be empowered by law to remove and eliminate from any country those deemed as undesirable or unsuitable as citizens of the New World Order. In other words all who will not accept his 'mark.' That is what the Bible tells will happen and our very survival will only be possible through our unwavering faith in God!.

How would this not open itself up to absolute total and rank abuse, where through corrupt government bureaucracies it would be possible to simply designate ones enemies as 'unsuitable' and have them removed?

Ezekiel 38.21 tells that this will be a time when... *against his own brother the sword of each one will come to be.*

22. *And I will bring myself into judgment ...*

23 *..and I shall certainly magnify and sanctify myself and make myself known among many nations.* God will act, as He most certainly will not tolerate a situation of total anarchy.

Again, Hosea 7.8 reads... *As for Ephraim...it is with the peoples* (of the nations) *he mingles*

10. T*hey have not returned to their God nor looked for him. ...Ephraim proves to be like a simple minded dove without heart.*

Simply because he does not know his (our) true identity and has been duped by the prevalent false notion of multiculturalism...the euphoria of the 'lets all get along fallacy' and all the compromising that is eroding his power, dumbing down his children, emptying his treasuries, lowering standards and turning his streets and cities into third-world ganglands, crime ridden, drug infested ghettoes and no go areas.

Surely, as a guest in the hosts country the least that would be expected is that the guest should try to abide and respect the prevalent standards, why should it be otherwise and yet that is exactly what is happening. It's that simple, the 'wicked one' has turned around all our good intentions to serve his own interests. In the process the West has let down its guard down and as a result 'Israel' - everywhere is being overrun by the nations.

So well has this situation been imposed that the slightest objection will immediately result in one being castigated as a racist bigot, such are the norms. But it is bigger than that. The type of hype that is being propagated and is designed to demolish and destroy our Western standards and values, is that there are no absolutes, just diverse cultures, lifestyles and that it is not for us to say what is right or wrong even in our own backyard as it were.

The family is one such value that has been under attack especially, the role of the father as family head, where this has been minimized and made inconsequential? Gone are the days where the principle of 'spare the rod and spoil the child' is followed. Instead the child is encouraged to report any such discipline to the authorities, which can result in the father facing imprisonment and his child being removed and placed into 'foster' care.

So in fact a system has been allowed to develop in Western society where the state actually has the power to destroy the home and the family, while the cultures of undeveloped countries are celebrated by such expressions as *'it takes a village to raise a child.'* While on the surface there is nothing wrong with that. There is however, silence about the fact that in such cultures the child's father rarely if ever takes responsibility for the proper raising of the child or providing for the family, resulting in many of the children literally becoming dependent upon others in the village for their sustenance. For as much as they are illegitimate orphans and beggars. It has been estimated that even in the 'land of plenty' the United States, that the illegitimacy rate among African - Americans is as high as seventy percent and that most of the resultant single parent homes are dependent on social welfare grants and payments. Malcolm X is recorded as saying that anyone could make babies, but that it took a man to be a father and to support and raise a family.

Notice how Israel's mixing with the nations was actually foretold in Daniel 2.32. where the immense image representing five World Powers in Nebuchadnezzar's dream was interpreted by Daniel...... *it's head was gold,* (Babylon)... *it's arms silver,* (Medes-Persians) *its belly and thighs were of copper* (Greece-Alexander the Great)

33. *Its legs were iron,* (Rome) *and notice its feet* (**the Anglo-American world power**) *were partly iron and partly clay.*

Notice verse 43. whereas you beheld iron mixed with clay, they will come to be mixed with the offspring of mankind (people from the nations); **but they will not prove to be sticking together......just as iron is not mixing with clay**.

So according to the Scriptures, diversity and multiculturalism is not going to work and will ultimately fail. Properly controlled and better managed perhaps it might have had a chance. But, by simply opening the 'floodgates' which has happened and is still going on through an Immigration agenda that we likely are not supposed to know about that, putting it mildly, will not have the desired effect.

Obviously, there can be no turning back, so it is the

consequences that will have to be faced. Our 'God' given gates have been left wide open and our countries are in the process of being over-run. We are undoubtedly in decline and descending from first world to third world status or to something in between. But this should not be surprise. We were warned that this would happen in the Scriptures. Deuteronomy 28.43,44, tells about us no longer being head and becoming the 'tail.' We were also warned that this would be only the start *of the pangs of distress*.

Interestingly, in the 45 Declared Declarations for The Communist Takeover of America, point number 43. reads ...'Overthrow all colonial government before native populations are ready for self-government.'

Call it 'Freedom, Liberation' get them high on expectations, let them leave the lands, flock to the cities and crowd into overcrowded unhygienic squatter camps and informal settlements to await the wave of the 'magic wand' that will bring them the rewards of free education, employment, housing, electricity, water, toilets and other services, healthcare... anything they want, they've got it,' so sing the politicians. Let them increase in numbers until they 'storm the bastille,' spill out and ravage, rape and plunder their way through the established cities, suburbs, business and industrial areas until at last they will 'have it all,' total freedom and equality with every vestige of civilization torn down and stripped bare. Then when there is nothing left for them to destroy, let them turn upon each other. Isn't 'freedom great?'

As regards the Western World in general, surely it should have been foreseen that by allowing an uncontrolled mass influx into the developed countries of unskilled, under educated people trying to escape the miseries of their former countries would only result in the transfer of all such misery to the host countries?

But clearly, that was the intention and can be seen in all the 'let's all get along' hype, the multiculturalism, affirmative action, white guilt and all the other stuff espoused by the Illuminati machinery. If that was not the case, why was it not allowed to take it's course naturally? Might it now be said that the tables have been turned, and **instead of what once was forced 'segregation' that there is now 'forced integration' as a prelude to the World Government where the World will be One! Yeah Right!**

For the 'wicked one' to succeed and to achieve his purpose, and win the argument and challenge against God's Sovereignty, he has to succeed in the destruction of Israel and to have everyone accept his mark.

By having everyone thus 'marked' will provide him with a great victory that will enable him, to be able to taunt God by pointing out that the ones that God once called 'His People,' by accepting his mark, would then have become his people (Satan's people) and would thus 'put it in God's face.' But, he knows that the battle would not be over and that God has many people across the earth who will never bow to him (Satan.) Thus Revelation 12.11 *they conquered him through the blood of the Lamb and the word of their witnessing, they did not love their souls in the face of death*!

Satan also knows that his time is at an end and God can act at any time to remove him and his kind. Thus the need to attack and destroy the nations and countries making up

Israel that will ensure his total control of the world. This he has been doing by infiltrating people from the nations in among us, in advance to 'soften us up' and take us off guard, before bringing in his crowd to finish the job and destroy us in what will be his third and final attempt.

What needs to be understood and has never been properly appreciated is **what makes third world and first world cultures so totally different**. It is simply that the Nations making up the ones referred to by God as 'My Chosen People Israel' use and abide by His laws, while those Nations outside the realm of Israel live by the laws **imposed on them by Satan**!

Our system operates primarily upon the principles of, Roman Dutch Law, which in turn are based upon Mosaic or God's Laws, otherwise known as the 'Ten Commandments.' **These are also referred to as Judeo- Christian values**.

While the laws and principles imposed by the 'wicked one' upon nations outside the realm of Israel essentially are *'the survival of the fittest*' a selfish *'winner takes all philosophy*' and that man is simply a carnal beast.

So in essence what is at play is a struggle between 'love, mercy' kindness and 'wickedness and evil,' Between God's way and Satan's and everyone, by having *'free will*' will be totally free to decide on which side to stand.

Also, it has nothing to do with Satan wanting to bring about a benevolent 'World Order Government' that will rid the world of all it's problems. It all goes back to the Universal issue about the challenge made against God's Sovereignty and 'Absolute' Right to Rule His Creation. That Creation cannot be ruled by <u>love and kindness</u>, as God would have, but rather by <u>selfishness and greed</u>. Also the principle of '***the survival of the fittest***,' that man is a carnal beast as contended by his Adversary. But God will finally settle matters and end the rebellion at last.

Looking at the big picture, after failing to bring the West down in two World Wars, the approach this time round is to try from within. It has been said, 'Destroy America's Middle-Class' and you've got America. Once you've got America, you've got the world. That is the real reason for all the hype about 'diversity'. <u>The '**wicked one**' has little or no regard for the masses and in improving their lot. To the contrary he would wish all humanity to be in that state and condition.</u>

Sadly, democracy in many western countries is simply a guise for socialism where the middle - class are being saddled with increasingly heavy tax burden to provide safety nets for the masses.

In theory the end of the cold war heralded the prospect of unprecedented peace, prosperity and growth for the world economy. During the nineties and well into the new century despite the events of 9/11/2001. The entire world economy took a giant step forward with real growth and prosperity everywhere in evidence.

There was even talk of the Dow going above the $20.000 mark. In retrospect it would seem that the growth was manageable and likely would have continued had the U.S. Federal interest rate not been raised some eighteen points in as many months by the newly appointed Fed Chairman. The 'wheels simply came off,' how else might it be described. When the rates eventually came off their 'highs' back down to more manageable levels, it was too late, the damage had been done and the collapse of the property market and the financial and banking crash that followed is now history.

Obviously, while there will always be some threat of inflation, surely it could not have been so great as to have warranted such extreme action. Certainly a more pragmatic approach might have been less crippling? Now with all trust blown out of the entire financial system, who can say where matters are headed as the world economy limps along.

In effect this has thrown the world's financial pendulum from one extreme to the other and it will take years for it to right itself. Precious time that the world's economy simply does not have and cannot afford if severe austerity is to be avoided.

The suggestion that the big banks need to be broken up, likely might also be taking matters in a wrong direction, although obviously there would be arguments to the contrary. Their only part in the entire debacle was having to trade the bad mortgages that were granted in terms of the U.S. 'Fair Housing Act Legislation,' where institutionalized lenders were required by law to make mortgages available to those who otherwise would not qualify.

These mortgages were then sold by banks to para-statal or quasi government entities like 'Fannie-Mae' and 'Freddie-Mac' who squandered billions buying up the paper that had been made worthless by the spike in interest rates that had brought about the recession and the resultant massive unemployment. The mortgages were bundled or packaged up as CDO's (Collateralized debt obligations) that were then traded on world markets. Had the interest rates not been increased so high and at a more moderate pace, the situation might have been avoided or have been less damaging.

Is it not simply 'mind boggling' trying to understand how Fed Chairman Benancke, by what might be described as his 'iron-fisted' increasing of the Fed rate by some eighteen points in as many months, failed to know or realize that in the process that this would bring down the banking system not only in America, but across the entire world where interests rates are all based or linked to the Fed rate? The reasons he offered at the time was that it had been done as a safeguard against a perceived threat of inflation, when in fact there was no threat of any major significance.

Also, in the circumstances would it not have been reasonable in the early stages of the 'rate hike' for former Fed Chairman, Greenspan to have given him a fatherly 'tap' on the shoulder and suggest that he ease up a little to see what effect the increases were having?

With that in his resume, how was it possible that he would then be allowed to continue to serve as Chairman of the Fed in the new Administration? Yet, not a word has been said about it!

The 45 Declared Communist Objectives For The Take Over America[56] that were written into the U.S. Congressional Records in 1963, clearly show that now all but one such objectives have been achieved. <u>It is only the establishment of an International World Government through the United Nations that remains to be achieved</u>. So, this is not conspiracy theory, but will soon become fact.

But there is always the hope that they will somehow 'Get It,' and finally see and understand the futility of Satan's

---

56   available on the web at www.rense.com

system and will turn around before it's too late. In fact, it should be our hope that enough intelligent thinking people will do likewise, and put aside short term political and other interests and work for what is for good and in the common interests of everyone? Are we not all in this together and can there be any doubt as to the absolute 'wickedness' of our common enemy.

It has always been Israel against the nations, Satan has throughout time been intent on destroying God's people to ensure his own victory and nothing will ever change that - it is that simple. Having failed in both World Wars to bring Israel down militarily, the 'wicked one' is now engaged, very subtly in a 'softening' up process of us the target. We are unknowingly being prepared, 'softened up,' disarmed and everywhere being made defenseless. Who knows it could even happen by 'blue helmeted' troops (thugs perhaps?) simply marching in under International Law, with those responsible for or security and protection powerless to do more than simple look on. When they come for us they will want us to go quietly.

Make no mistake, Satan knows exactly what he is doing and if we let him he will succeed and because of the 'free will' issue God will not intervene. By rejecting God as ruler we will only bring about our own destruction. But He does however, warn us in advance by providing us with all the facts (what you are now reading) through His Word, but we are the ones who must decide.

However, for most, when the New World Order Government does come, besides the usual hype that accompanies all such major events and happenings, when nothing out of the ordinary happens and everything gets back to normal, most will likely take that attitude, "what was all the fuss about, by all those religious fanatics preaching Armageddon and all the other stuff?" Which is understandable, but again it's all about deception!

Like stubborn children and by ignoring our Maker's Handbook, <u>we are unable to see where our independent spirit has led us</u> and here is the point, how we have and will continue to play right into Satan's hands, so effective are his deception's.

In this way it is likely that the majority will be conned into believing that everything is ok and will view the taking of 'the mark of the beast,' as no 'big deal,' and in this way they will have allowed themselves to be deceived into foregoing their only hope of eternity.

Thus the 'SEEK HIM EARLY MESSAGE.' If enough people with heartfelt sincere prayers and petitions were to make their voices heard by their truly loving Heavenly Father, it will indeed 'soften His face' and those days will be cut short. For any who are not sure about how to go about this and how to pray? Consider an excellent example found in Daniel chapter 9.verses 3 to 21 where Daniel's prayer's about a very similar situation Israel was facing back are recorded for our benefit. Notice verse 3...*I proceeded to set my face to the true God, in order to seek (him) with prayer and with entreaties.*

NO PLACE FOR RELIGION IN THE NEW WORLD ORDER

All religion (religion around the world) will be closed by the political system as brought out in Revelation 17.16....<u>*and the ten horns....and the wild beast....will hate the harlot and will devastate her and ...completely burn her up with fire.*</u> So, forewarned is forearmed so that when it happens it need not come as a surprise.

Chapter 18.2....reads....She has fallen! Babylon the Great has fallen.

4. GET OUT OF HER 'MY PEOPLE' (the churches)....if you do not want to share in her plagues. In verse 23 we see the identity of her....

23. And no light of lamp will ever shine in you again, and <u>no voice of a bridegroom or of a bride</u> will ever be heard in you again because by your spiritistic practice all nations have been misled. There should be no doubts or arguments about who this refers to, the Bible is very clear on the matter!

Notice, also that the warning is directed to 'My People' those making up the vast numbers of God's chosen or covenant people Israel - the 'lost sheep.' Who were part of Israel long before they ever became part of the Church.

By infiltrating and corrupting the church Satan has very subtly ensnared and imprisoned millions upon millions, including the ones God calls 'My People.' While the laity believe that they are giving worship to God, by the use of imagery and idols they are in fact worshiping Satan. One example would be the very prominent 'IHS' symbols seen in churches that actually represent 'Isis, Horus, Set' the **ancient Egyptian sun god**, so subtly is the deception and it is all around us! Satan needs the entire world to bow down to him. That is what this is about

Sadly, America today is Protestant in name only, with the leadership of its mainline churches having already capitulated to Rome in ways not even apparent to their members! Such is the deception.

That Britain and America despite being victorious down through history against Satanic onslaughts and more recently in Two World Wars and should now capitulate and surrender their God given sovereignty to this very same force that has repeatedly tried destroy them is simply unconscionable. God forbid that it will happen!

In Christ's early church there were no divisions and there never should have been any. Which only goes to show how the 'wicked one' has successfully manipulated all religion using his 'divide and rule' strategy to achieve his own purposes. Again, 'Peace on Earth' and Goodwill to all men is not something that has ever been on his agenda. Yet rarely if ever is the blame for all the evil that surrounds us laid squarely at his feet where it rightfully belongs.

AGAIN, THIS IS NOT ABOUT KNOCKING ANYONES FAITH OR RELIGIOUS BELIEFS, AFFFILIATIONS OR THE CLERGY. THE PROBLEM IS NOT WITH THE MEMBERS, BUT RATHER WITH SATAN AND THOSE DOING HIS BIDDING. HOW LONG WILL IT BE FOR THINKING PEOPLE START TAKING NOTICE OF WHAT IS GOING ON AND REMOVE THEMSELVES FROM RELIGION THAT HAS BEEN CORRUPTED BY THE 'WICKED ONE' AND HEED THE CALL FROM HEAVEN, 'TO GET OUT OF HER, 'MY PEOPLE!' AGAIN, IT'S ABOUT FREE WILL AND UNDOING THE DECEPTIONS OF THE 'WICKED ONE' WHO HAS 'DECEIVED,

MANIPULATED AND INFILTRATED RELIGION TO ACHIEVE HIS OWN PURPOSES! CLEARLY, DELAYING WOULD BE FOOLISH AS CLEARLY THERE ARE LIMITS EVEN TO GOD'S PATIENCE!

THE HAPPY ENDING!

HOW GOD WILL FINALLY DEAL WITH 'HIS PEOPLE?'

In Hosea 7. 8 ...we read ...*Ephraim has mingled among the nations.9. strangers have eaten up his power....Also, gray hairs have become white on him...*

11 *Ephraim proves to be like a simple minded dove....*But at Hosea

11.1. We read... "*When Israel was a boy, then I loved him and out of Egypt I called my son."* ....

3....*I taught Ephraim to walk taking them upon my arms....*

9. "*I shall not bring Ephraim* (BRITAIN) *to ruin.....for I am God not man, the Holy One in the midst of you."*

Notice Ephraim's response as recorded in Hosea 14.8 "*Ephraim will say. ' What do I have to do any longer with idols*?"

Indeed how much better it would be if it were not only Ephraim, but in fact all those who are in anyway enmeshed or entrapped in the entire Illuminati network and are in some way involved in putting together the New World Order. Would it not be great if they also were to come to their senses and realize that while it will happen, that the World Order Government is doomed and as foretold in the Bible that it will simply have been an exercise in futility that will cost each one their eternity? *Calamity will put the wicked one himself to death.* Psalm 34.21 Is this the destiny you seek? But, again this about *Free Will* and only you can decide.

Know that it is God's will....*that all sorts of men should be saved and come to an accurate knowledge of the truth.* 1 Timothy 2.4 Know also that the battle has already been won – *they did not love their souls even in the face of death* Revelation 12.11. God can end matters at any time. Notice Matthew 24.22....*for the sake of the elect those days will be cut short.* Know also that ...*Whenever they are saying; "Peace and security!" then sudden destruction will be instantly upon them.*....1 Thessalonians 5.3.Likely, just when they think that all their well laid plans are coming together, God will act and bring it all to nothing!

So, you are encouraged *'to get out of here,'* to get out of any form of worship not approved by God, any religious organization not telling you this and be part of those spoken of in Isaiah chapter 2.2....*And it must occur in the final part of the days* ...

7. many will come and say "Come, you people and let us go up to the ...House of the God of Jacob and He will instruct us in His Way. He will set matters straight respecting many people. And they will have to beat their swords into plough shears and their spears into pruning hooks and they will learn war no more!" For the former things have passed away... Revelation 21.1

www.ingramcontent.com/pod-product-compliance
Lightning Source LLC
Chambersburg PA
CBHW070454090426
42735CB00012B/2552